DEAN CLOSE SCHOOL

LIBRARY

This book must be returned by the latest date stamped below.

"Cambridge is a stimulating setting for any writer or artist, offering as it does academic debate and architectural splendour, ancient tradition and high tech invention, institutions that are quintessentially English and yet act as a magnet for visitors/scholars from all over the globe. In my Laura Principal novels, the vibrant pulse of the city that has looped itself around the ancient colleges becomes almost another character. Any admirer of Cambridge will be drawn to this collection of watercolours by distinguished artists in which the colleges are so vividly and affectionately evoked."

Michelle Spring
Cambridge

author of "In the Midnight Hour", winner of the Crime Writers of Canada award for Best Novel of the Year

For FRAZER, GRAHAM, JEREMY, LORRAINE and RACHEL

First published in Great Britain in 2004 by

CONTEMPORARY WATERCOLOURS LIMITED
165 Parrock Street
Gravesend
Kent DA12 1ER
Tel: 01474 535922
Website: www.contemporarywatercolours.co.uk

Set in Garamond. Artwork by Janet Davie. Project co-ordinator: Susan Grant

Printed by Gros Monti, Ashford, Kent

ISBN 09526480 2 4

Front cover: **King's** *- Main Entrance (Dennis Flanders)*
Back Cover: **Sidney Sussex** *- The College Gatehouse (John Doyle);* **Peterhouse** *- Trumpington Street (Dennis Flanders)*
   Gonville and Caius *- From King's Parade (Jane Carpanini);* **Downing** *- Main Court (Ken Howard);* **Clare** *- Bridge (Dennis Roxby Bott).*

CAMBRIDGE WATERCOLOURS

*Views of the university and colleges by members
of the Royal Watercolour Society*

Jane Carpanini   John Doyle   Dennis Flanders
Ken Howard   Dennis Roxby Bott

Text by

MALCOLM HORTON

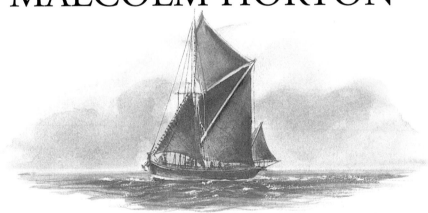

CONTEMORARY WATERCOLOURS

The Royal Watercolour Society

The Royal Watercolour Society (RWS) was founded in 1804 and received its Royal Patronage in 1884. In February, 2004, it celebrated its bicenterary with a visit from H.M. Queen Elizabeth II and is the oldest Society of its kind in the world. Society Members have included Peter De Wint, David Cox, Helen Allingham, John Sell Cotman, Samuel Palmer, Sir Edward Burne Jones, John Singer Sargent, Arthur Rackham, Sir William Russell Flint and Charles Knight.

The Society is now based at the Bankside Gallery which is situated on the South Bank of the River Thames overlooking St. Paul's Cathedral. It was opened on 11th November, 1980 by Her Majesty the Queen. The area is of great historical importance, and is now the focus for the best contemporary art with the opening of the new Tate Gallery of Modern Art. There are some 90 Members of the R.W.S., both Fellows and Associates and admission to the Society is determined by annual Election.

Jane Carpanini, R.W.S., R.W.A.

Jane was born in Bedfordshire in 1949 and was elected to the Royal Watercolour Society in 1978, establishing a reputation for expansively composed and meticulous watercolours. She was trained at Brighton College of Art and the University of Reading.

Her work is in the collections of the National Library and National Museum of Wales. She is also a member of the Royal West of England Academy and the Royal Cambrian Academy, and exhibits regularly within these societies. She has served as the Vice President and Honorary Treasurer of the Royal Watercolour Society.

In 1983 she was the winner of the prestigious Hunting Group's Prize for the Watercolour of the Year by a British Artist.

John Doyle, M.B.E., P.P.R.W.S.

Born in Dulwich, London, in 1928 John is a past President of the Royal Watercolour Society and has had many exhibitions in major galleries in London and Canterbury Cathedral. A book, entitled "An Artists Journey Down the Thames", was published in 1989.

He has recently undertaken a peripatetic journey retracing and painting in St. Augustine's footsteps from Rome to Canterbury to celebrate, in 1997, the fourteenth hundredth anniversary of this famous event. This culminated in an exhibition at Canterbury Cathedral of the 300 or so paintings made in the course of the journey.

John now lives on the edge of Romney Marsh in Kent and readily acknowledges the help and encouragement he received in the early years from the distinguished painter John Ward.

Dennis Flanders, R.W.S., R.B.A.

Born in London in 1915 Dennis was unquestionably one of the greatest pencil and watercolour artists of the twentieth century. He attended evening classes in antique drawing at the Regents Street Polytechnic whilst working for a firm of fashionable interior decorators. He painted the scenery and architecture of the British Isles for over sixty years before his death in 1994.

He has been called the "Canaletto of our time" by Peterborough in the 'Daily Telegraph' and was, for some years, a graphic reporter with the 'Illustrated London News' and his pictures of London during the Blitz are treasures of the Guildhall Library and the Imperial War Museum.

A Freeman of the City of London, he was a member of the Art Workers Guild and served as Master in 1975. Two previous books have been published containing the body of his lifetimes work, "Britannia" in 1984 and "Watercolours in Academe" in 1994.

Ken Howard, R.A., R.W.S., R.W.A.

Ken was born in London in 1932 and is a member of the Royal Academy and Royal Watercolour Society. He is also President of the New English Arts Club, that bastion of figurative painting and drawing. He was official war artist in Northern Ireland in 1973 and 1978.

Since his National Service in the Royal Marines 1953-55 he has had a close association with the British Army, undertaking special commissions for them throughout the world, including portraits of the Royal Family. Ken's work is held in public collections including the Imperial War Museum, Ulster Museum, National Army Museum and the Guildhall Art Gallery.

He has studios in London and Cornwall and two books on his life and works have been published entitled "The Paintings of Ken Howard" in 1992 and "Ken Howard A Personal View" in 1998.

Dennis Roxby Bott, R.W.S.

Born in Chingford, Essex, in 1948, he attended the prestigious Norwich School of Art where he studied fine art painting and obtained a Dip.A.D. (Fine Art). He was elected to the Royal Watercolour Society in 1981.

Dennis, who now lives in Sussex, has had regular one man exhibitions in London and Sussex notably Ebury Street Galleries, SW1, Worthing Art Gallery and Museum, Lannards Gallery Billingshurst and the Ogle Galleries.

He is a regular exhibitor at the annual spring and autumn Royal Watercolour Society exhibitions at the Bankside Gallery and in 1992 he was a prize-winner at the annual Discerning Eye Exhibition at The Mall Gallery in London. His commissions include the Wardroom of H.M. Royal Yacht Britannia, Sotheby's, American Express and the National Trust.

CONTENTS

Foreword

by

The President of the Royal Watercolour Society 1996 - 2000

The colleges of Oxford and Cambridge are something very special, nothing quite like them exists anywhere else in the world. They are not monastic but have an unmistakeable affinity with monasticism, they are not churches but have deep religious roots, their libraries, halls, chapels and cloisters are of un-surpassing beauty. They are steeped in history but still remain relevant. These enchanting, dreamy exteriors are misleading for behind the seemingly peaceful atmosphere of the cloister, they are power-houses of contemporary thought; in economics, science, philosophy, politics, an amalgam of old professors, young ambitious fellows and youthful learning.

In producing the images in this book, we, the painters and you who look at our pictures, owe a debt to Malcolm Horton for reminding those of us who know them and for introducing those who do not, of their enduring loveliness.

I am very proud to have been included in the fortunate group of painters who have contributed to both "Oxford Watercolours" and its companion publication, this book "Cambridge Watercolours". All of the artists are fellow members of the Royal Society of painters in watercolours - the "R.W.S." and it is appropriate that it is published in the year 2004, the bicentenary of the foundation of the Society, the oldest such body anywhere in the world. We represent a long line of watercolour painters; Joshua Cristall, Peter De Wint, John Varley, John Sell Cotman, David Cox, Sir William Russell Flint and many others all practising in a medium which is a quintessentially British genre.

May you who read this book and look at its pictures get as much pleasure out of doing so as we the painters experienced in creating them.

John Doyle, M.B.E., P.P.R.W.S.
Warehorne, Kent
May 2004

Introduction

In 1815 Rudolph Ackermann published his prestigious "History of the University of Cambridge, its Colleges, Halls and Public Buildings".

The book was illustrated with watercolours produced by a team of artists, who were amongst the finest topographical draughtsmen of their day, Augustus Pugin, William Westall and Frederick McKenzie. The Cambridge book was a companion volume to his Oxford book of a similar name produced a year earlier. The books were a huge success and did much to promote the reputation of British watercolour painting. Since Ackermann's time nothing of a more contemporary nature has been produced and, it is our humble intention, with the publication of "Cambridge Watercolours", to rectify this omission.

Although the watercolours reproduced in this book are associated with particular colleges, they are inextricably linked to Cambridge the City and, of course, Cambridge the University. All students are members of a college which hosts them during their time in Cambridge. The college selects them and, thereafter, accommodates them, feeds them and supervises their studies.

The genesis for this collection of watercolours is the series of limited edition prints of Cambridge colleges which my company, Contemporary Watrercolours, has produced over the past fourteen years, under the generic title *Contemporary Cambridge*. Most have started life as joint projects with the colleges featured, and all have appeared regularly in the University magazine CAM.

At the outset it was decided that quality and the pursuit of excellence were to be our watchwords. The watercolour medium was selected because it best suits the topographical nature of the subject matter - fine drawing being a prerequisite. To demonstrate our intentions to the world at large, it was decided that we should commission only artists who were members of the Royal Watercolour Society.

It is difficult to believe that the Borough of Cambridge did not attain the full title and dignity of a city until March 1951, 800 years after Oxford. This, despite the fact that Cambridge is a very old town, *Camboritum* in Roman times and *Granterbridge* in Saxon days. It received a Borough Charter from King John in 1201 and its first university chancellor was elected in about 1246. However, because of its location, away from the pathways of kings and armies on their way to London, Cambridge has always been essentially provincial. In the view of many, Cambridge is pre-eminent in Britain as a city of fine architecture and beauty and I trust the paintings in this book reinforce this view.

Finally, I would like to thank the group of talented artists who have produced the pictures in this publication. It has been a rare privilege to work with some of Britain's most eminent watercolourists. Thanks are also due to the Fellows and Heads of House of the colleges represented in this book for their support and encouragement.

Malcolm Horton
Tutt Hill , Kent

CHRIST'S COLLEGE

Dennis Roxby Bott

First Court

Christ's College was first established as God's House in 1437 by William Byngham, a London Parish Priest, for training grammar schoolmasters. They were encouraged to read for the lesser degree of Master of Grammar and so replace the huge number of teachers killed by the Black Death.

They were in effect the successors to the ancient and disteemed class of students called Glomerels who aspired no higher than to acquire a smattering of Latin so that they could become schoolmasters. They lived *hand to mouth* having no permanent abode and were often forced to beg. They were answerable to the Master of Glomery a post which had become an antiquated curiosity by the fifteenth century and disappeared altogether in 1540.

When Henry VI began building King's in 1448 his site clearance involved moving God's House from its riverside location to the site now occupied by Christ's College on St. Andrew's Street. Like many of the older foundations in Cambridge, however, it was not sufficiently endowed and through the good offices of the ubiquitous John Fisher, Bishop of Rochester, Lady Margaret Beaufort's help was enlisted. In 1505 with a Royal Charter from King Henry VII (her son) the college was re-founded as Christ's College with Lady Margaret as its foundress.

There still remain a few buildings from the God's House period, principally those between the Great Gate and Chapel in the First Court. Clearly visible in the painting opposite is the Hall built during the later time of Lady Margaret and exhibits the typically Tudor oriel window. The earlier God's House buildings, not visible in the painting, are diagonally opposite the Hall to the left. All of the buildings in the First Court from both periods were constructed of clunch, an inferior local chalk based material which has a proclivity to early deterioration. From 1714 onwards, therefore, it was necessary to reface these buildings with limestone from Rutland.

Among Christ's distinguished alumni was Charles Darwin the nineteenth century biologist and author of "Origin of the Species". John Milton, the puritan poet, author of "Paradise Lost" was at the college from 1625 to 1632 and in the Fellows Garden is Milton's Mulberry Tree. This is the only survivor of a group of trees planted in 1608 (the year of Milton's birth) to boost the English silk industry.

In the twentieth century Christ's produced several notable writers. C. P. Snow, author of the quintessential Cambridge novel, "The Masters" (part of the "Strangers and Brothers" series of novels) was a fellow of the college from 1930 to 1950. William Cooper, who was at Christ's in the early 1930s was the author of "Scenes from Provincial Life" thought by many to be the seminal influence on the new breed of "irreverent" post-war English writers including Osborne, Braine, Sillitoe and Bradbury. More recently Colin Dexter graduated from Christ's in 1953 and paradoxically went on to glorify Oxford through his creation, Inspector Morse.

CHRIST'S COLLEGE

Dennis Roxby Bott

Main Gate

The late fifteenth century saw many early institutions falling into decay particularly Michealhouse (later to be absorbed into Trinity) and God's House. John Fisher, Bishop of Rochester, had been a student of God's House and enlisted the help of Lady Margaret Beaufort to convert it into Christ's College. Margaret was the mother of Henry VII and a devout and pious woman, whose influence on intellectual and spiritual life was pervasive. In 1497 she chose as her confessor John Fisher and together this formidable pair founded not only Christ's but also St. John's.

Christ's College was founded in 1505 and was richly endowed by Lady Margaret Beaufort. She was an extremely wealthy woman having outlived four husbands and was as a result Countess of Richmond and Derby. She had only one child, Henry, who had become King, so she had no family calls on her fortune. Indeed she spent remarkably little on herself and used her wealth for educational and other charitable purposes. This thrift and modesty was expressed by her wearing a hair shirt next to her skin and in place of regal fineries she wore modest robes much like a monk's habit. She established, both at Oxford and Cambridge, the first endowed professorships in Divinity which we now call the Lady Margaret Professorships. John Fisher was the first holder of this position in 1497 followed in 1511 by Erasmus who was then residing at Queens College.

Christ's College codes, like St. John's, contained in its statutes a provision that half of the students should be drawn from the northern parts of England, then in a minority at Cambridge. Fisher, himself, was a northerner born in Beverley, Yorkshire.

In Dennis Roxby Bott's painting of the Main Gate the coat of arms of the Beaufort family can be seen, also the motifs of the Lancastrian red rose and portcullis much used by the Tudor dynasty. Above the coat of arms is a statue of Lady Margaret which was added in 1888.

CHURCHILL COLLEGE

College Front   *Jane Carpanini*

After his retirement as Prime Minister in 1955 Sir Winston Churchill visited the Massachusetts Institute of Technology (MIT). He was so impressed that he suggested that such an institution be founded in Britain whose primary purpose was to train scientists for research and development and which forged links between industry and academe.

After talks with Government academics and American foundations it was decided to found Churchill College which would be a national and Commonwealth memorial for one who had, as the Appeal prospectus puts it, "earned the gratitude of the English-speaking peoples". A Board of Trustees was appointed with Sir Winston as its titular head and had amongst its members representatives from academe, industry and the Trade Unions. In 1958 an Appeal was launched and handsome donations were made by the Ford and Rockafellor Foundations as well as the Transport and General and Amalgamated Engineering Unions. By 1966 £5 million had been raised (about £60 million in today's terms). Forty-two acres of farmland were acquired from St. John's College half a mile to the west of the city centre on the Madingley Road. Twenty-one architectural practices were invited to enter a competition for the design of Churchill College. It was perhaps the most important single architectural competition in England of the post-war period and was won in July, 1959 by Richard Sheppard. The architecture is unashamedly modern. Its rhetoric corbusian. Its fidelity, however, to the collegiate idea is demonstrated by the warm vernacular Stamford stone brick and the intimate ten interlocking courtyards. Sir Nikolaus Pevsner the distinguished architectural historian judges Churchill *"an outstanding conception, the best of the new"*.

The College obtained its Charter and its first post-graduate students in 1960 followed, in October, 1961, by its initial intake of under-graduate students. Against the background of Churchill College's "brave new world" there was unleashed one of the great intellectual battles, so beloved by academics, over the need for a chapel in a college whose scientific Fellows were largely agnostic or atheist. It led, in 1961, to Francis Crick, the DNA pioneer resigning his Fellowship and to propose to Sir Winston Churchill that the college would be better served by a brothel. He also enclosed a cheque for ten guineas towards such a project. His cheque was returned without comment. In the end a compromise was reached with the help of Lord Anthony Beaumont, an Anglican priest and Liberal politician, who agreed to finance the entire cost of a chapel. A trust was set up which leased from the college a small piece of land on the periphery of the college site on which a chapel would be built. In words of a former Vice Master of Churchill, Mark Goldie, "there is a chapel at Churchill College, but there is no Chapel of Churchill". Even Crick compromised and accepted an Honorary Fellowship in 1965.

It is fair to say that Churchill's architectural style presents the topographical artist with a real challenge. Jane Carpanini demonstrates in the painting opposite her unique ability to deal sympathetically with less romantic architectural styles.

CLARE COLLEGE

Dennis Flanders

Old Court

Originally founded as University Hall in 1321 its establishment was inspired by the foundation of Oxbridge's earliest college, University College Oxford, in 1249. It was Cambridge University itself which obtained the licence to found the college and its Chancellor, Richard Bardew appropriated two messuages (dwelling house with attendant land) for this purpose. The messuages were part of the land given to the University in 1270 by a physician, Nigel de Thornton and forms the present site of Clare.

In 1338 with the college facing financial ruin, Richard de Bardew persuaded a wealthy heiress, Elizabeth de Burgo Countess of Clare, to act as a "white knight" and save the college. She was a grand-daughter of Edward I and sister-in-law to Piers Gavaston (close friend of Edward II) and she had been widowed three times before she was 30. She was as a result a very wealthy woman and well able to secure the colleges future with generous endowments. As a result Richard de Bardew ceded all his rights to Elizabeth Countess of Clare. She built the college, obtained its first statutes and not unnaturally renamed it Clare Hall and was henceforward reckoned to be its foundress. It was renamed Clare College in 1856 and is in effect Cambridge's second oldest college still extant.

The Countess of Clare was the first in a distinguished line of noble ladies to found Cambridge colleges in the late mediaeval period. She was followed by the Countess of Pembroke (Pembroke College) Henry VI's wife, Queen Margaret of Anjou (Queens' College), Henry VII's mother Lady Margaret Beaufort (Christ's and St. John's) and Lady Francis Sidney (Sidney Sussex).

Dennis's painting opposite is a view looking eastwards across Old Court towards the Porter's Lodge which, contains two gateways, one on the inside and one on the outside of the Court. Although the fundamental motif of the eastern range of buildings, dating from 1638, is classical the two gateways have an exuberant baroque style incorporating an oriel window. To the right, the south range of buildings contains, in the centre, the Latimer Room which is used for conferences and meetings. It is named after Hugh Latimer, Bishop of Worcester, a Fellow of the college, who was burnt at the stake, in Oxford in 1555, on the orders of the Roman Catholic Queen Mary I. The reason for his execution along with Bishop Ridley and Archbishop Cranmer were their alleged Protestant heresies.

Bernard Flanders. — Clare.

CLARE COLLEGE

Dennis Roxby Bott

View From Clare Bridge

Clare's is the oldest bridge in Cambridge still extant and was designed by Thomas Grumbold and completed in 1638. It marked the beginning of what was the complete reconstruction of Old Court and also the beginning of an association with the Grumbold family of builders. Thomas Grumbold had received a fee of three shillings for the bridge design but it was his nephew Robert who completed the rebuilding of the Old Court between 1638 and 1719. The homogeneity of design in the buildings is unequalled in Cambridge. However, all building work was stopped in 1642 due to the Civil War and was not recommenced until 1662. The college's building materials were commandeered by the Parliamentarians for the defence of Cambridge Castle. Oliver Cromwell as Lord Protector, however, eventually made payment for them in the sum of £400.

The decision to build a completely new court was brought about by congestion due to increased student numbers and dilapidation due to the poor quality of building materials used in the original mediaeval court. The material used had been clunch (hard chalk) and the only building stone native to East Anglia. In the seventeenth century, however, it was decided to use probably the best building material in the world, limestone. This was obtained from the famous oolitic limestone quarries of Weldon and Ketton in Rutland. The slates are from the equally renowned and neighbouring Colley Weston. The warmth of the yellow limestone and the proximity of the great lawn of King's College explain why the outer south side of Clare's Old Court is one of the most photographed buildings in Britain.

Dennis Roxby Bott's painting opposite shows both the bridge and the western range of the Old Court with the chapel of King's College rising above in the background. This view could only have been painted in winter as the buildings would have been obscured by summer leaves, a topographer's nightmare.

CORPUS CHRISTI COLLEGE

Dennis Roxby Bott

Old Court

The college of Corpus Christi, founded in 1352, differs in its origins from any other college at Cambridge or Oxford. It had no patrician founder emanating as it did from Town rather than Gown. It was the outcome of the combined action of two craft guilds - of Corpus Christi and of the Blessed Virgin Mary. The members of these two guilds wished to found a college for the education of secular priests (not ordained) who should be charged with the duty of praying for the souls of deceased members.

It was originally known as St. Bene't's College because it used the adjacent St. Bene't's Church as its college chapel, until 1579 when Sir Nicholas Bacon, Keeper of the Great Seal of England, agreed to build a new one. St. Bene't's Church remains today the oldest building in Cambridge, dating from 1025 and dedicated to St. Benedict.

Many of the two guilds' brethren lived in the parish of St. Bene't's and pulled down certain tenements belonging to them in what is now Free School Lane and built on the site the picturesque Old Court. It helps explain why Corpus Christi is the sole college to have its site in the heart of old Cambridge. Old Court dates from 1350 and is the first and oldest complete court or quadrangle in either Cambridge or Oxford.

Two of Corpus Christi's most famous alumni are linked by the enduring Canterbury connection. Matthew Parker was Master 1544 - 1553 and became the second protestant Archbishop of Canterbury in 1558. It was he who created two scholarships at St. Bene't's for pupils of King's School Canterbury. One of the earliest recipients was Christopher Marlowe 1564 - 1593, undoubtedly the greatest of Shakespeare's predecessors and whose involvement in espionage on behalf of his country may have led to his early death. In the early part of the twentieth century a portrait was discovered in an attic and dated 1585 with the legend "this was him in the 21st year of his age". It is presumed to be that of Marlowe and today hangs in the Hall.

CORPUS CHRISTI COLLEGE

Dennis Roxby Bott

New Court

The 1579 chapel of Corpus disappeared in 1823 to make room for William Wilkins's New Court and new chapel. Wilkins had a string of successes to his name at this time including, in Cambridge, King's College entrance screen, Downing's classical masterpiece and in London, the National Gallery and University College. Corpus, however, was Wilkins favourite project and he built a crypt for himself under the College Chapel where his body still rests.

New Court includes Archbishop Parker's Library seen to the right in Dennis Roxby Bott's picture. It is one of the most famous college libraries anywhere and is the beneficiary of Parker's assiduous saving of notable books and manuscripts at the time of the dissolution of the monasteries.

Amongst the most obvious treasures are the illuminated Gospel Book used by St. Augustine in his missionary campaign among the English in 597 A.D. It is the manuscript on which by tradition each new archbishop of Canterbury takes his oath of office. Also in the collection is Alfred the Great's own copy of the Anglo Saxon Chronicles and the earliest records of the English language.

It also contains the oldest cookery book in the country belonging to Matthew Parker's wife. It has recently been edited by the present Master's wife, Mrs. Anne Ahmed, and its publication in 2002 was sponsored by the Worshipful Company of Cooks.

The college changed its name from St. Bene't's to Corpus Christi at the time William Wilkins built New Court in 1820 and the Old Hall, with its oriel window seen on the previous page, became the college kitchens. In Dennis Roxby Bott's painting opposite can be seen to great effect the "new" Chapel on the left and Parker's Library on the right. The effect was enhanced by Dennis using artistic licence and moving the lamp-post in the foreground to give a better balance to the picture. The contrast between Old Court and New Court is perfectly illustrated in Dennis Roxby Bott's two vivid paintings.

DARWIN COLLEGE

Dennis Roxby Bott

The Hermitage and Newnham Grange

After the Second World War it became increasingly clear that Cambridge needed a new wholly graduate college. In 1962 Oxford had responded to a similar need by founding Linacre College. In 1963 three Cambridge colleges, Gonville and Caius, St. John's and Trinity, announced their intention of founding a graduate college. As a result Darwin College was founded in 1964 and housed in Newnham Grange, the former home of the Darwin family (descendants of Charles Darwin of "Origin of Species" fame), in Silver Street on an attractive part of the River Cam, near the old Mill Pool and Weir. Additionally a neighbouring house, The Hermitage, was acquired from St. John's College. Before The Hermitage became the property of Darwin College in 1964 it had, since 1954, housed the fledgling college of New Hall, Cambridge's third female college. New Hall moved to its own purpose built site in 1964. This move was facilitated by the generosity of the Darwin family who gifted land on the Huntingdon Road, half a mile north of the city centre.

Darwin College is unique amongst Cambridge colleges possessing an island of its own. In fact, two islands, little island and big island. Their formation is due to the fact that the River Cam divides just above Newnham Grange, the left fork being known as the River Granta. It flows for just over half a mile southwards before rejoining the River Cam.

In Dennis Roxby Bott's painting The Hermitage is the building to the left of the copper-beech and Newnham Grange is on the right as viewed from the bridge between the islands. They are linked by the Rayne Building, here obscured by the copper-beech tree, and the result of generous benefactions from the Rayne Foundation, which was set up by Lord (Max) Rayne, whose magnificent portrait by Graham Sutherland dominates the college dining hall, which his Foundation also funded. From humble beginnings in East London he became a successful property developer. He was also a generous supporter of the theatre, opera, ballet and architecture and was for many years Chairman of the Board of The National Theatre. He died in October, 2003.

The Darwin family has continued to support the college by lending many family portraits which adorn the walls of the main public rooms and in enabling the college to purchase the fine alabaster bust of Erasmus Darwin, Charles's grandfather. The founding colleges have also continued their support of and interest in Darwin.

Kirby Bolt

DOWNING COLLEGE

Ken Howard

Main Court

The seventeenth and eighteenth centuries saw the rise of no new colleges in Cambridge . After the foundation of Sidney Sussex College in 1596 the next foundation was Downing College in 1800. The reason almost certainly was the Reformation. The monastic spoils were dissipated and the wealth of the dignitaries of the mediaeval church was unknown to their married protestant successors. The Stuart kings had neither wealth nor will to endow learning.

The foundation of Downing College came about through most unlikely and fortunate circumstances which the founder, Sir George Downing, could not realistically have expected. He was the grandson of Sir George Downing, the first baronet, a diplomat and soldier who had served both Cromwell and Charles II. He is perhaps most famous as the builder of No. 10 Downing Street, home of British Prime Ministers.

Sir George was born in 1685 and was to inherit his grandfather's fortune. He married his cousin Mary when she was 13 and he 15 but they never lived together. He never forgave her for becoming Maid of Honour to Queen Anne. Sir George would never have legitimate issue so he left his estate successively to four cousins, who all died without issue. Sir George, however, provided for what must have seemed an unlikely scenario by stipulating that in the event of his legatees dieing without issue, his estate was to be used to found a college in Cambridge.

Sir George died in 1749 and the sole surviving cousin Jacob in 1764. However, Jacob's widow and her second husband would not relinquish the estate and there then ensued 36 years of debilitating legal battles. In 1800 the Court of Chancery decided in favour of Sir George's Will and George III granted Downing College a Royal Charter.

Grandiose buildings in the Grecian style were proposed which were to surpass all its predecessors and in size its quadrangle was to exceed that of the Great Court of Trinity. William Wilkins was appointed as architect but he only completed between 1807 and 1820 the west range and part of the east range including the Master's Lodge and Hall. At this point the money ran out and it was not until 1873 that further money was found to complete the northern part of the east range.

Wilkins's design, instead of creating enclosed Courts, spaced out the college buildings and in effect produced the first campus some years before the first campus university at Virginia.

Ken Howard's painting opposite undertaken in the late Autumn of 1994 captures the spaciousness and park-like setting of Downing's Main Court with the Hall in all its Grecian glory, partially visible on the left of the picture and the Master's Lodge to the right.

[27]

DOWNING COLLEGE

Ken Howard

View from Kenny Gate

The architect William Wilkins's early nineteenth century grand design for Downing was not fully realised until the twentieth century due to shortage of money. What had seemed an adequate endowment was sadly depleted by costly litigation concerning the disposition of Sir George Downing's estate.

The twentieth century, however, saw the piecemeal completion of this uniquely campus-style college with its fine trees and park-like setting.

In 1931 Sir Herbert Baker designed four residential blocks which were placed on the north side of the quadrangle. The money for this development came from the sale to the University of 12 acres around Lansfield Road. The north side was completed in 1950 when Baker's partners Scott and Hebling completed a simple but lovely chapel which was inserted between Baker's earlier residential blocks.

Architects Scott and Hebling also designed two blocks of rooms which were erected in 1959 and 1961 largely paid for by the two daughters of Professor C. S. Kenny, a very distinguished Law Fellow, who is also commemorated by the Kenny Gate in Tennis Court Road.

In 1987 there began a period of new building which really did complete the Downing project and at the same time reinforcing the integrity of William Wilkins's classical style. The architect responsible for this continuity was Quinlan Terry who firstly designed the Howard Building which contains the JCR (Junior Common Room) and a fully equipped flat floor concert and meeting room. He also designed Howard Court and both are named after a member of the college, Dr. Alan Howard, whose generosity made both possible. Another notable design by Quinlan Terry is the impressive Maitland Robinson Library named after another generous benefactor who was a Downing graduate. The Library was opened on 22nd November, 1993 by H.R.H. The Prince of Wales.

In Ken Howard's painting opposite the Howard Building is on the right, and beyond the north range building on the left can be seen the tower of Quinlan Terry's library. Ken's painting brings out the beauty of the yellow and pink tints contained in the Ketton stone of which all but the early eighteenth century Portland stone east range were constructed. Also, Ken Howard's wonderful use of light, his trademark so to speak, is beautifully demonstrated in this picture.

EMMANUEL COLLEGE

Dennis Roxby Bott

Front Court

Emmanuel was founded in 1584 on the site of a former Dominican Priory by Walter Mildmay, Chancellor of the Exchequer to Elizabeth I. He was a Puritan of the most zealous type who wanted his college to be a seed-bed of learned men for the new Protestant Church. Emmanuel rapidly became the principal centre of Protestant theology in Cambridge.

However, in the 1630's the college was subject to religious persecution during the high-church revival under Charles I and Archbishop Laud. So much so that many of its Puritan graduates went in voluntary exile to New Town Massachusetts. Amongst their number was John Harvard who by his benefactions gave his name to the first American University. New Town Massachusetts was renamed Cambridge as a compliment to an Emmanuel preacher, Thomas Shepherd.

As so often in England during the sixteenth and seventeenth centuries the religious pendulum swung back. In fact during the Civil War the President of Queens' and 20 fellows were ejected by Cromwell for showing royalist sympathies and replaced by seven good protestants from Emmanuel. The process of outing was repeated in most of the other Cambridge Colleges and in the period 1644-1650 all but one of the 16 College Heads were replaced by puritans with six of their number being supplied by Emmanuel.

Roxby Bott's painting opposite uses the entrance arch to Front Court to frame Sir Christopher Wren's chapel built between 1668-1673. The choice of architect was made by William Sandcroft who had been Master of Emmanuel before becoming Dean of St. Paul's and later (1678) Archbishop of Canterbury. He had already been negotiating with Christopher Wren with regard to the rebuilding of St. Paul's Cathedral after the Great Fire of 1666. Knowing that Wren had built the Chapel at Pembroke College, Cambridge in 1665 and was in the process of completing the Sheldonian Theatre in Oxford he was keen to get Wren's commitment to the St. Paul's project. What better inducement than to award him the commission to design Emmanuel's chapel which was completed in 1673.

EMMANUEL COLLEGE

Dennis Roxby Bott

New Court

New Court in some ways is a misnomer of Walter Mildmay's 1584 foundation. However, when it was built in 1825 it replaced the original Court with its ornamental gateway which fronted onto Emmanuel Street. It had already been replaced as the principal Court with the building of Front Court in the seventeenth and eighteenth centuries with its entrance onto St. Andrew's Street.

Emmanuel was founded on the site of a former Dominican Priory closed by Henry VIII at the time of the Reformation. New Court, however, still contains significant parts of Mildmay's original buildings. In Roxby Bott's pretty painting can be seen, to the right his Hall with its oriel window, a typical Elizabethan feature. At right angles to the hall and to the left of the arch which leads from Front Court is the Old Library building. This was a controversial building in as much as it was originally Mildmay's chapel built with a north-south orientation instead of the usual east-west and it was never consecrated. This snub to the convention was more to do with Mildmay's fanatical puritan sympathies. With the completion of Christopher Wren's chapel in the Front Court in 1672 the old Chapel became the College's Library and it remained so until replaced in 1931. It is now used as a very elegant conference and social function facility.

Also seen to great effect in the picture are the box hedges which enclose a noted herb garden and two of Emmanuel's ubiquitous "academic" ducks waddling purposefully back to their mediaeval pond in the college Paddock, no doubt having just received their *honoury* D.A.s! Incidentally this pond, like the one in Chapman's Garden is fed by the seventeenth century Hobson's Conduit, (see Peterhouse - View across Trumpington Street) and was originally the fishpond of the old priory.

GIRTON COLLEGE

Dennis Roxby Bott

College Front

Cambridge was in 1869 the first residential University in Britain to open its doors to women students. In that year with the encouragement of university authorities Emily Davies established Britain's first residential college for women in Hitchin Hertfordshire. Its location, however, proved to be impractical with Cambridge lecturers having to commute between Hitchin and Cambridge on a regular basis. A compromise solution was found in 1872 when sixteen acres of land was purchased near the village of Girton, 2¹/₂ miles north of Cambridge town centre. This location was thought to be near enough for male lecturers to visit but far enough away to discourage male students from doing the same.

Alfred Waterhouse designed the first buildings in red brick Tudor Gothic style in the traditional college form with a chapel and hall but he introduced the idea of bed-sitting rooms on corridors instead of the usual vertical staircase. The students moved to Girton in 1873 and in 1887 the architect's son, Paul, designed the imposing gatehouse with its octagonal corner tower in the same Tudor Gothic style adopted by his father. Interestingly grandson Michael completed Woodlands Court in the 1930s, thus showing that

nepotism can sometimes work for all concerned. Alfred Waterhouse's other architectural gems include Manchester Town Hall and the front and tower gatehouse at Balliol College, Oxford.

The rather forbidding aspect of the red brick buildings is offset by the very beautiful and extensive grounds, now 50 acres in area. Girton's gardens are very large, even by Cambridge standards, and includes the Old Orchard planted in 1893 which contain 40 old and rare varieties of apple tree; the highest number in private ownership. There are also 21 numbered specimen trees including *Ginkgo biloba* and *Lirodendron tulipifera*. Altogether Girton's gardens embrace Emily Davies's founding vision of the right environment for the education of women.

Dennis Roxby Bott in his somewhat unusual perspective of Girton's entrance and chapel has softened the dominance of the gatehouse and given a suggestion of the promise which the gardens hold.

GONVILLE and CAIUS COLLEGE

Jane Carpanini

Caius from King's Parade

Originally founded as Gonville Hall in 1348 it was the second of four colleges founded during the 50 year reign of Edward III (1327-1357). Pembroke, Trinity Hall and Corpus Christi were the others. The college grew out of the household established by Edmund Gonville in Free School Lane, close to where Corpus Christi was later founded

Edward Gonville, its first founder, was a parish priest from Norfolk who died after only three years in 1351 leaving a foundation but no money. His friend and Executor, William Bateman, Bishop of Norwich, had a year earlier founded Trinity Hall and moved Gonville's foundation into two existing houses close to his own college. As executor of Gonville's will he ensured that sufficient monies were available to enlarge and endow the college and gave to it, in 1353, its first statutes. Without Bateman's crucial intervention it is doubtful whether Gonville Hall would have survived. It was never a wealthy college and needed re-founding in 1557 by one of its former

undergraduates, John Caius (pronounced keys) a wealthy physician. In effect it had three founders, although only Gonville and Caius are eponymous. Initially the college did not have sufficient money for new buildings so existing houses on the site were converted to collegiate use. A very small chapel was built in 1393 but it was not until 1490 that its First Court was completed known as Gonville Court. This was also very small being only 26m square. The original chapel can be seen in the painting of Caius Court on the next page, to the left with an arch leading to Gonville Court. It does not look mediaeval because like many Cambridge Courts it was entirely refaced in the eighteenth century and now has a neat classical appearance.

Jane Carpanini's painting opposite shows the public face of Caius which was designed in 1869 by Alfred Waterhouse. It is very much in French Renaissance style and includes behind the facade the very pretty Tree Court. Also visible to the far left, with its pediment, is part of the University Senate Building.

GONVILLE and CAIUS COLLEGE

Jane Carpanini

Caius Court

Gonville Hall had by the 1540s attained a modicum of financial stability due to a bequest of the Physick hostel on the other side of the street, now called Trinity Lane, which doubled the college's accommodation. But in the 1540s Henry VIII took it over as part of his foundation of Trinity College. The site of the hostel is now part of the Great Court of Trinity. Until recently the college still received a small annual ground rent from the Treasury. However, the viability of Gonville Hall was now at risk with its accommodation severely depleted. A White Knight was needed and he duly arrived in the personage of Dr. John Caius.

John Kaye entered Gonville Hall as a student in 1529 (he was to later Latinise his name to Caius) and became a fellow of the college before leaving Cambridge in 1539 to study in Padua for four years. He travelled extensively before returning to England to set up a medical practice in London. Such was his success that he was elected President of the Royal College of Physicians and professionally attended Edward VI, Mary I and Elizabeth I successively. It was with the permission of Mary I he re-founded his old college and renamed it Gonville and Caius College. He drew up new statutes, made large gifts of money and land and extended the college buildings. On the southern end he built a new court, the present Caius Court. It was the first example of a three sided court whose purpose was to have one side open to allow air to circulate.

Caius created three classical stone gates representing Humility, Virtue and Honour. Humility where the Porter's Lodge stands on Trinity Street, Virtue connecting Tree Court to Caius Court and finally Honour on the formerly open south side of Caius Court. It is through the Gate of Honour that Caiusans process to the Senate House to receive their degrees. His gates were very much in the Italian Renaissance style which he had admired in Italy. From Padua on a more prosaic level he imported the new science of Anatomy and Caius was undoubtedly the catalyst for medicine being recognised among Cambridge studies.

In Jane Carpanini's painting opposite the Gate of Virtue is in the centre of the picture whilst the Gate of Honour with its unusual sundials is to the far right.

HOMERTON COLLEGE

Ken Howard

The Great Hall

In 1976 Homerton became an approved college of the University of Cambridge. It had, for the previous eighty-two years, existed in Cambridge as an institution for teacher training. Its history, however, began in 1768 in the pleasant little village of Homerton on the edge of Hackney Marsh, then in Middlesex.

Homerton Academy was established by the Congregational Fund Board to educate ministers for the non-conformist Congregational Church. It was one of 35 such flourishing academies set up towards the end of the eighteenth century whose curriculum included the modern subjects of history and mental philosophy, not taught in the Universities of Oxford and Cambridge. In 1823 it changed its name to Homerton College and not long after, with the foundation of London University whose curriculum included "modern subjects", it effectively became redundant.

It was at this point that Samuel Morley who was Treasurer of both Homerton College and the Congregational Board of Education decided that Homerton was to become a voluntary institution for the education and training of teachers. He implemented his changes in 1852 and in effect Samuel Morley was the founder of the new teacher training college.

By the 1890's Homerton College had become surrounded by factories which were thought to be neither conducive to health nor learning. In 1894, therefore, the Congregational Board of Education decided to move Homerton College to Cambridge. To this end it purchased for £15,000 the ten acre site and newly erected buildings of the failed Cavendish College, founded by the Rev'd. Joseph Brereton in 1876 with the aim of making university education available at an affordable price, particularly to the farming community. Times were not propitious in the farming industry and Joseph Brereton was not a good financial manager. Cavendish College closed in 1891 overwhelmed by debt.

In Ken Howard's vivid painting opposite can be seen the original Cavendish buildings, particularly the impressive hall with its rose window and fleche, erected in 1889 and financed to the tune of £10,000 by the Duke of Devonshire and G. E. Foster, the noted Cambridge banker.

At the time of its move to Cambridge, Homerton was a mixed college consisting of 100 women and 38 men which was not to the liking of the Department of Education who insisted that men be excluded. Men were not admitted again to Homerton until 1976, at the time it gained collegiate status. Interestingly Homerton's Coat of Arms contain large elements of the Morley family Coat of Arms thus acknowledging its debt to Samuel Morley.

Ken Howard

JESUS COLLEGE

Jane Carpanini

First Court

The open courts set in spacious grounds distinguish Jesus from all other Cambridge colleges. They are an inheritance from the twelfth century Benedictine nunnery of St. Mary and St. Radegund. By 1496 it was clear to the Bishop of Ely, John Alcock, that Radegund's had degenerated morally, spiritually and had fallen into disrepair. It was in terminal decline and reduced to two nuns, one of whom had a somewhat dubious reputation. Therefore, in 1497 Bishop Alcock obtained from Henry VII a licence to dissolve the Nunnery and to found a college.

The great church of St. Radegund whose tower we see in the background of the painting opposite was adopted for college use. It is one of the most interesting pieces of early mediaeval architecture remaining in Cambridge today. The quality and scale of its thirteenth century workmanship are up to cathedral standards. Later additions include a roof by Pugin, windows by

Burne Jones and Madox Brown and a painted ceiling by William Morris. Jane Carpanini's painting is taken from a similar perspective as the one by William Westall in Ackermann's Cambridge book of 1815. It shows buildings of three distinct periods from the thirteenth century range in front of the chapel tower, the fifteenth century buildings to the right of the gate tower and finally the seventeenth buildings to the left. The Chapel range contains the Upper Hall and Old Library which have been adapted from the original nunnery buildings. First Court, however, preserves a continuity of style despite its diverse origins.

Interestingly the south transept of the chapel has a memorial to Archbishop Cranmer, a Jesus undergraduate, who later became the first Protestant Archbishop of Canterbury and who was burned at the stake in Oxford by Mary I in 1556.

JESUS COLLEGE

Jane Carpanini

The Chimney and Gate-Tower

With the evidence of the stranded leviathan of King's College before his eyes the founder of Jesus in 1496, Bishop Alcock, was keen not to lay down a burden of unrealisable expectation on his college. What was dilapidated he rebuilt; what was unnecessary he adapted to other uses. Whatever combined beauty with utility he reverently conserved. He was, after all, comptroller of the royal works and buildings to Henry VII and his architectural skill and taste are evidenced by his work at Ely and Malvern. He also built a new gate-tower which was unlike others of the period such as Queens', Christ's, St. John's and Trinity. These were by their square massiveness and corner turrets suggestive of defence whereas Alcock's tower is all elegance and spirituality and in the centre of which his statue now stands. The gate-tower is approached by a long, narrow high walled path called *The Chimney*, to the right of which can be seen the oriel windows of the Master's Lodge.

The college's earliest statutes were given to it by Alcock's successor at Ely, Bishop Stanley, and are remarkable in that they uniquely, at the time, make provision for teaching within the walls of the college. Also they allude to the teaching of grammar to boys once the province of the older inferior class of student called Glomerals (see page 10).

A twentieth century Master of the College, was Arhtur Gray who had earlier entered Jesus as a student in 1870. In 1926 he wrote an absorbing book called "Cambridge University An Episodical History", to which the author of this book is greatly indebted as a source of largely forgotten aspects of University history.

KING'S COLLEGE

Dennis Flanders

Main Entrance and Front Court

After the frenetic activity in college foundation which occurred during the first half of the fourteenth century, when seven new colleges were created, the following ninety years saw only two new foundations before King's in 1441. There were two principal reasons for this reduced activity. The plague or Black Death which waxed and waned continually during this period and reduced the population of England by over a third (1¼ million) and the ruinously expensive Hundred Years War with France.

Henry VI, in this matter at least, was decisive. He would found a college which would be designed by him and would be the grandest in scale and beauty. Eton which he had founded a year earlier was to be a twin foundation with King's and for four hundred years only Etonians were admitted. It was modelled on existing arrangements in Oxford and Henry had no doubt intended to found his new college there. However, the spiritual climate then prevailing in Oxford was uncongenial due to the polemical writings and heresies of John Wycliffe and others.

The University authorities in Cambridge were not happy with the discriminatory nature of Henry's new foundation which was quite unparalleled in its history. Further disquiet was caused when statutes granted his students special privileges. They were awarded degrees without sitting university examinations and were not subject to the discipline of the University authorities. It was not until 1873 that non-Etonians were admitted. Today, in contrast, King's takes a higher proportion of State educated students than other colleges.

Henry VI's grand design for his college was carried out fitfully and only manifest itself, albeit magnificently, in his wonderful chapel which was completed sixty nine years later during the reign of Henry VIII. Apart from the hastily constructed Old Court nothing else happened for nearly three hundred years. The Wars of the Roses had put paid to Henry VI.

The college was finally completed in the eighteenth and nineteenth centuries as the painting opposite identifies. To the left beyond the grass is part of the Fellows Building, designed by James Gibb in 1723 in a simple classical style. He also designed the Senate House which can be seen on the far right in the picture. The busy college front with its entrance screen and impressive gatehouse which separates the college from King's Parade was designed by William Wilkins in 1824. Finally the founders statue can be seen above the fountain where it was erected in 1879.

KING'S COLLEGE

Dennis Flanders

Chapel Interior

The two paintings of King's which appear opposite and on the previous page show the exterior and interior of Cambridge's chief glory, King's College Chapel, considered by some the most outstanding building in Britain and certainly the finest example of the wholly English perpendicular style.

These two paintings appeared in Dennis Flanders's book "Britannia", published in 1984 and he commented at the time "It is either the exterior or interior of a building that gives the greatest pleasure. In this case, however, it seems that a miracle has been achieved for both are equally splendid". It is the only part of Henry VI's grandiose scheme for his Royal foundation which came to fruition and saved it from being a mere chimera. Begun in 1448, the fabric of the building was not completed until 1513 due to lack of money and the Wars of the Roses. Also limestone used for the building was not available locally being imported initially from Yorkshire and then Rutland. The master mason, from 1506 until completion, was John Westall, who also designed the Bell Harry Tower of Canterbury Cathedral. Westall was probably responsible for the breathtaking fan vault which can be seen in the picture and is the largest in the world. The glazing of the twenty six windows, perhaps the biggest single job of its kind hitherto attempted was financed by Henry VIII using his own glaziers. The oak screen and organ case seen in the centre of the picture was also provided by Henry VIII and carries his initials as well as those of Anne Boleyn, his Queen from 1553 to 1556.

The painting opposite was one of forty nine featured in an exhibition of Dennis's work held in Cambridge in 1980. The exhibition was called "*Sursum Corda*" which means lift up your hearts. A very appropriate title as far as this work is concerned.

King's has a world famous choir which since 1918 has taken part in the Festival of Nine Lessons and Carols broadcast around the world from the chapel every Christmas Eve.

ALL VISITORS are REMINDED
that THIS
IS A PLACE OF WORSHIP
AND SO TO
MOVE ABOUT QUIETLY
AND OUT TO THINK
EXCEPT IN A LOW VOICE

KING'S COLLEGE

Jane Carpanini

View from the Backs

The painting opposite perfectly illustrates a unique feature which Cambridge possesses. The Backs are a lovely renowned expanse of trees, lawn, pastures and gardens situated behind the riverside colleges and imbue Cambridge with a pastoral air quite unlike Oxford. The Backs are particularly beautiful in springtime when carpeted by crocuses, daffodils and tulips.

The many college bridges which span the Cam are another outstanding feature of Cambridge and King's was the first college to have a bridge, although the present bridge seen to the right of the picture is not the original.

The area of land shown in Jane Carpanini's painting, in the fifteenth century represented the heart of Cambridge. It linked the river with the market place and was the busiest part of mediaeval Cambridge. Henry VI's ambitious plans for King's, however, involved the clearance of this in 1441 which practically took the heart out of the town and caused profound indignation amongst the townspeople.

The pity of it was that this widespread devastation did very little to advance the King's aims, because of the lack of money and will the site remained empty for three centuries and sheep grazed where men had once dwelt and trafficked.

In the centre of the picture can be seen James Gibb's Fellows Building of 1724, the first serious attempt to begin the construction of the Front Court. Also to the right in the picture, just over the bridge, is Bodley Court (1889 - 1893) an "L" shaped block of chambers by G. F. Bodley, situated between the Provost's Lodge and the river.

The grassed area shown in Jane's picture is known as Scholars Piece and in season cows are allowed to graze on its rich pasture: thus reinforcing the pastoral image of Cambridge.

MAGDALENE COLLEGE

Dennis Flanders

River Court

In the painting opposite is captured a quintessential Cambridge scene of punting on the Cam below Magdalene Bridge. To the right, on the opposite bank, is part of the mediaeval brickwork of the river-facing range of Magdalene's Old Court dating from the 1470s.

Originally founded as Monk's Hostel in 1428 by Abbot Lytlington of Crowland Abbey near Peterborough, it was a Benedictine educational establishment and was supported by the abbeys of Ely, Ramsey and Walden. In 1470 the building of the First Court was commenced with money provided by Henry, second Duke of Buckingham. It was around this time that the name of the establishment was changed to Buckingham College and secular students were also admitted.

The political flood which swept away the monasteries at the time of the Dissolution and at onetime threatened to absorb the colleges had begun to ebb in 1542. The monks resident in the college had departed in 1539 and in 1542 Henry VIII rewarded his loyal Lord Chancellor, Thomas Baron Audley,

by making him a gift of Buckingham College. He inherited a college where the buildings were of collegiate pattern, containing hall, chapel, offices and chambers, all in decent repair. Thomas Audley re-founded the college in 1542 as The College of St. Mary Magdalene. So mean, however, was the provision left for it by Audley in his Will that when he died in 1544 Magdalene was destined to struggle to survive for centuries.

Sadly he is best remembered by many as presiding over the trials of Sir Thomas More, John Fisher, Bishop of Rochester (co-founder of St. John's and Christ's) and Anne Boleyn.

The dead hand of the founder, however, was heavy on his small foundation. The mastership was to be forever in the gift of the possessor of the estate of Audley End into whose ownership Audley crept after the dissolution of Walden Abbey. The present owner and descendant of Audley, Lord Braybrook still exercises the right to appoint Magdalene's Master.

MAGDALENE COLLEGE

Dennis Flanders

Magdalene Street

This painting which uniquely captures the essence of the domestic architecture of mediaeval Cambridge, was one of three commissioned by Dr. David Cooper, a distinguished sometime Fellow of Magdalene (1977-1982). He is now an eminent transplant surgeon at the Harvard Medical School in the United States. The other two commissions are The Pepys Building and River Court, which also appear on adjoining pages.

In the picture, in the distance on the right, can be discerned the pub sign of the sixteenth century Pickerel Inn, a busy and popular hostelry, much used by the student population. The main entrance to Magdalene is on the left, just before the Pickerel Inn.

Magdalene Street is situated just inside the entrance to mediaeval Cambridge at the foot of Castle Hill, where the main routes from the north, east and west converge. Both sides of the street are now owned in the most part by the college. It is now a row of picturesque shops but was formerly a slum, notorious for its many brothels! Today, however, the rooms above the shops have been converted into student accommodation. Behind the buildings on the right is Benson Court, one of three Courts built in this area between 1925 and 1970 which house the majority of the student population (the other Courts are Mallory and Buckingham).

Benson Court is named after perhaps Magdalene's most celebrated Master (1915-1925), A. C. Benson, who had been a Fellow from 1904. He raised the prestige and profile of the college from a sickly, under-provisioned establishment of only 45 students and Fellows to a total of 460 today. His facile pen produced essays, literary criticisms and the words of "Land of Hope and Glory", enabling him to freely open his purse to act as the catalyst to the impressive college building programme that followed, including Benson Court, designed by Sir Edwin Lutyens (1869-1944).

MAGDALENE COLLEGE

John Doyle

The Pepys Building

Originally constructed in the late seventeenth century it became known as New Building. It was only with the arrival of the Samuel Pepys library in 1724 that it gradually became known as the Pepys Building. It is for this reason, as well as its architectural merits, that it is Magdalene's jewel and one of Cambridge's loveliest landmarks.

In the earlier part of the seventeenth century what was envisaged was a modest all brick building in two wings with only a skeletal link between them. By the late 1670s, however, as no work had started due to lack of finance, the advice of Robert Hooke was sought. Hooke was a collaborator with Christopher Wren in his London work after the Great Fire and is considered to be the founder of modern structural engineering. His big new idea was to create a series of rooms over a loggia to link the two wings. The project was revived with generous financial contributions being made by several graduates including Pepys and the then Master, Professor James Duport. It is clear that at this stage in the late 1670s there is no evidence of his intention to bequeath his library to the college. It is only in a codicil to his Will, two weeks before his death on 26th May, 1703, that he finally makes a disposition of his library in Magdalene's favour.

What is an enigma and a dichotomy rolled into one is the difference between the back and front of the Pepys Building; the back is like a Jacobean manor-house, whilst the front is neo classical in Ketton limestone from Rutland (it is the only part of the college not in brick). The inscription above the central arch says *Bibliotheca Pepysiana 1724* and above that is carved the Arms of Samuel Pepys and his motto *Mens cujusque is est* (the minds the man).

Pepy's library consists of 3,000 volumes housed in twelve oak book cases designed by him. Included in the collection are mediaeval manuscripts, early printed books by Caxton, Sir Francis Drake's nautical almanac and Pepys's own diaries between 1660 and 1669.

The system of shorthand Pepys used in his diaries was devised by Thomas Shelton and published in 1647. Pepys entered Magdalene as a graduate in 1651 and would have learned Shelton's shorthand system known as tachygraphy, at that time. This shorthand system, however, was quickly superseded by other methods and when, in 1820, the St. John's graduate The Reverend John Smith embarked on the laborious task of deciphering Pepys diaries Shelton's system was unknown. He spent years on his task before discovering amongst the Pepys library Shelton's 1647 instruction book!

Samuel Pepys led a very high profile public life, being a Member of Parliament, Secretary to the Admiralty and President of the Royal Society. In short he was well connected. This is why his diaries are so interesting. These, along with the rest of his library, can be viewed by the public at set times.

MAGDALENE COLLEGE

John Doyle

The Hall and Gallery

The Benedictine Order had founded Monks Hostel in 1428 on a site which today comprises the area of the First and Second Courts. They utilised a few pre-existing houses which sufficed for a time but they did not erect fresh buildings of their own. A benefactor was badly needed. One appeared in the person of Henry Stafford, second Duke of Buckingham who between 1470-1472 in collaboration with John de Wisbech, Abbot of Crowland, planned First Court and began building the chapel. As a result of the Duke's patronage the name of the institution was changed to Buckingham College. Unfortunately "Buckingham's Rebellion" against Richard III resulted in his execution for treason in 1483.

The next important development was not until 1519 when Henry Stafford's son, Edward, the third Duke of Buckingham, built the Hall. His patronage, however, was short-lived because he was executed for treason in 1521 under somewhat dubious circumstances. The reason seems to have been his aristocratic disdain for the lowly born Cardinal Wolseley, Henry VIII's Chancellor. Henry did not impede Wolseley's revenge because it conveniently removed a potential threat, because the Staffords were of Plantagenet lineage and also Yorkist's. It is an irony that his father was executed for plotting against the Yorkist Richard . It was another twenty years before another potential patron arrived in the personage of Thomas Baron Audley (page 52) although his only contribution was to change the name of the college to Magdalene.

Edward Stafford's early sixteenth century hall was not significantly altered in size and fenestration (arrangement of windows) although the flat ceiling with garret rooms above was added in 1714. The double staircase and gallery were part of the 1714 renovation. The Fellows' Combination Room leads off the gallery, which is unusual in a Cambridge College where it normally leads off the hall dais. This was not possible in Magdalene's case because the chapel overlaps behind the dais. Another unique feature of Magdalene's hall is the fact that there are still no electric light fittings, so it is lit only by candlelight.

John Doyle was extremely keen to produce a painting of this unusual hall, particularly the idiosyncratic door fitting which gives the door a somewhat lopsided setting, as though viewed after passing round the port.

NEW HALL

Jane Carpanini

Fountain Court

In 1948 the University authorities belatedly made it possible for women to become full members of the university (Oxford had acceded in 1919). Many women M.As. felt it was time to provide more women with the opportunity of a university education. It must be remembered that only two colleges at this time admitted women (Girton and Newnham) so a third foundation was badly needed.

Accordingly in 1952 the Association to Promote a Third Foundation for Women in Cambridge was set up. By 1954 £25,000 had been secured and a postal ballot of Association members had produced a name New Hall. The new college was opened in October, 1954 with 16 graduates in the Hermitage on Silver Street which is now part of Darwin College (see page 24). By 1962 a total of £220,000 had been received from the Wolfson Foundation and the Elizabeth Nuffield Foundation. Additionally, the Darwin family (descendants of Charles Darwin of "Origin of the Species" fame) generously gave the college a gift of land up on the Huntingdon Road, half a mile north of the city centre. The college authorities appointed as architects the firm of Chamberlain Powell and Bon and as their first President, Miss Rosemary Murray. The new site was opened in June 1965 by Queen Elizabeth the Queen Mother.

The visual impact of New Hall is defined by the magnificent domed dining hall which seems to rise from the waters of Fountain Court. The concrete petalled dome was, with its Byzantine connotations, designed by Peter Chamberlain to echo Corbusier's landmark chapel at Ron Champ in France.

Completed in 1965 and now a Grade II listed building it was the precursor to Chamberlain's more famous work that concrete masterpiece that is the Barbican Centre in London.

One quite unique feature in the dining hall is the serving bar which rises up through the opening floor like a scene from "Star Trek". Still in good working order it is only activated on special occasions.

New Hall is definitely one of the architectural gems of Cambridge with its Byzantine dome and buildings of white brick and pre-stressed concrete.

NEWNHAM COLLEGE

Jane Carpanini

Sidgwick Hall

Quite rightly historians have identified the great contribution made in the cause of female education by Emily Davies at Girton and Ann Jemima Clough at Newnham. It was, however, a man, the radical moral philosopher Henry Sidgwick, who truly lit the fire when in 1869 he founded the Association for Promoting the Higher Education of Women in Cambridge. Cambridge University was at this time cautiously favourable to the cause of women's education and instituted a local examination for women over 18. It was seen as a qualification for governesses and school teachers. However, it soon became clear that a residential house was needed where female students could stay whilst studying. Consequently in 1871 Sidgwick persuaded Ann Jemima Clough, sister of poet Arthur Clough, to take charge of a house in Regent Street for this purpose.

The new institution briefly moved to Merton Hall (now the School of Pythagorus) before acquiring its own site, west of the River Cam where Newnham College was opened in 1875 with Miss Clough as its first Principal. In 1876 Eleanor Balfour (sister of the future Prime Minister) married Henry

Sidgwick and became Vice Principal of Newnham in 1880. She was to succeed Miss Clough as Principal in 1892 and in a sense she was with her husband the virtual founders of Newnham College.

Unfortunately, for the cause of women's education, relationships between Girton, the first female college, and Newnham, the second, became strained. Emily Davies, the Head of Girton, was a hard-liner who despised Newnham for its willingness to compromise with the University authorities over the question of equality with male undergraduates. Cambridge, however, was becoming increasingly hostile to women's education and when a ballot of all Cambridge M.As. was finally taken in 1897 it went overwhelmingly against admitting women to degrees. Although women were, after 1919, awarded titular degrees, it was not until 1947 that women finally achieved equality and were allowed to become full members of the University. October 1948 saw Queen Elizabeth the Queen Mother become the first woman to receive an honorary degree.

NEWNHAM COLLEGE

Jane Carpanini

Clough Hall

Newnham College was the architect Basil Champney's finest work and is a celebration of English eighteenth century architecture of the so called *Queen Anne style* of which Champney's was an ardent admirer. His buildings at Newnham, with their Dutch gables and sparkling white paint, were constructed between 1875 and 1910 and have been described as having a harmony and a gracious sweetness which have made them continuously admired, both in Cambridge and the world at large.

The first building, Old Hall, was completed in 1875 and following a suggestion from the college's first Principal, Miss Clough, it was designed along the corridor system instead of the usual vertical staircase arrangement. The first college to adopt the corridor arrangement was Keble College in Oxford. Newnham, however, now has the longest corridor in Britain linking all parts of the college.

In 1880 Sidgwick Hall was completed, followed by Clough Hall in 1887. The latter received much praise and was described as "one of the most charming and festive buildings" and the Builder magazine thought it "an exceedingly pretty bit of collegiate architecture" adding that the exterior of the dining hall with its two great oriel windows "is Gothic architecture carried out with Classic details". One could scarcely better this as a summary of the spirit of the Queen Anne style.

Newnham is still today a female-only college and it possesses the first college building in Cambridge to be designed by a woman, the Fawcett Building by Elizabeth Whitworth Scott in 1938. She was, in fact, the grand-daughter of the celebrated and ubiquitous Victorian architect, Sir George Gilbert Scott and the cousin of Giles Gilbert Scott the architect responsible for Cambridge University Library, Battersea Power Station and the red telephone box.

Jane Carpanini in the painting opposite has managed to capture both the classic details of the architecture and also the complementary attributes of the gardens which make Newnham so unique.

PEMBROKE COLLEGE

Dennis Roxby Bott

Old Court

In a six year period between 1347 and 1352 and during the reign of Edward III no less than four new colleges were founded Pembroke, Gonville, Trinity Hall and Corpus Christi. As with Clare the second Cambridge foundation, Pembroke the third was founded in 1347 by a noble lady in association with a University Chancellor on a site owned by the University. Pembroke was founded by the widowed Countess of Pembroke, Marie de Valence, who had married Aymer de Valence, Earl of Pembroke, when she was only seventeen. He was fifty and died of apoplexy three years later.

The original college statutes granted by Edward III contain a provision that preference should be given to students of French birth who have studied at an English University. It was a bridge building exercise by King Edward, who having triumphed the previous year at Cressy was keen to extend his influence to include French minds as well as their lands.

Pembroke is the first college to have a specially built chapel (1355) for its own exclusive use. Earlier all contemporary colleges appropriated the nearest convenient church. This structure was demolished in 1690 as it had been rendered redundant by the completion of Christopher Wren's chapel, in 1665, to the south of Old Court. The old chapel was replaced with a brick built library.

Pembroke had the smallest court of any college in Cambridge measuring only 55 feet by 95 feet. In the nineteenth century, however, Old Court was greatly enlarged with the demolition of the south range of buildings which had the effect of incorporating Wren's new chapel into Old Court.

The only parts remaining of the original college buildings are the gateway into Trumpington Street and the range between the Old Library and kitchen which can just be seen centre right in Roxby Bott's painting, next to the Old Library's perpendicular windows. Incidentally in the background can be seen the tower of the Pitt Building, part of Cambridge University Press and named after British Prime Minister William Pitt the younger, who was a student at Pembroke from 1773 to 1780.

PEMBROKE COLLEGE

Dennis Roxby Bott

College Front

In the picture opposite can be seen the western range of Pembroke's buildings which front onto Trumpington Street. Holding centre stage, so to speak, is the "new" chapel completed in 1665, from a design by Christopher Wren. Its impressive classical temple facade with a pediment and four Corinthian pilasters announces to the world that here is the first classically styled chapel in Cambridge. The Gothic style of the freemason builder is replaced by the travelled architect, who borrows his design from the palaces of the Italian nobles.

Pembroke chapel is, except for a doorway in Ely Cathedral, the first architectural design by Christopher Wren, who was at this time aged 30 and Savilian Professor of Astronomy at Oxford. For this seminal moment in history we are indebted to an inspired act of nepotism by Wren's uncle, Dr. Matthew Wren, Bishop of Ely, who had been a Fellow of Pembroke many years before. Matthew Wren had been imprisoned in the Tower of London for eighteen years by the Puritans and to celebrate his release in 1660 he decided to set about building a new chapel for his old college. He was not without experience in such matters because he had already built, 30 years earlier, the Jacobean Gothic chapel at Peterhouse where he had been Master. He no doubt felt that by appointing his relatively inexperienced nephew he could retain a degree of artistic control. Christopher Wren's other designs in Cambridge are the Chapel at Emmanuel and the Library at Trinity.

Among Pembroke's distinguished alumni are the protestant martyr Nicholas Ridley and the poets Edmund Spenser (author of the "Faerie Queene") and Thomas Grey (author of the "Elegy in a Country Churchyard"). In 1773 William Pitt entered the college aged fifteen. He left in 1780 and within three years he was Prime Minister.

PETERHOUSE

Dennis Flanders

The Old Court

Peterhouse is the oldest foundation in Cambridge and proudly declaims the appellation *College*. It's foundation in 1284 by Hugh de Balsham, Bishop of Ely, took place 35 years after that of Oxford's senior foundation, University College.

Hugh de Balsham was concerned at the hardships and deprivations facing clerks and scholars in thirteenth century Cambridge. The Bishops of Ely were already patrons to the Augustinian Hospital of Saint John's, whose doors were open to the poor and sick. He, therefore, arranged for the distressed scholars to be given asylum in the Hospital of St. John's. There was, however, much dissension between brethren of the hospital and the scholars and as a result the scholars were transferred to two houses next to the church of St. Peter. Balsham's endowments for the future maintenance of the scholars included the two houses and the church with its tithes and alter dues. On his death, in 1286, he bequeathed 300 marks (£200) to his scholars who bought more land and built a hall which survives to this day and is the oldest serving college building in Cambridge. It was heavily restored in the 1870s and has windows by Morris, Burne Jones and Madox Brown, which are reckoned to be amongst the finest pre-Raphaelite stained glass in Britain.

The Norman church of St. Peter gave the college its name but in about 1340 it fell down and when it was reconstructed was dedicated to St. Mary. It was only in the early nineteenth century that the college became known simply as Peterhouse. The church, however, was used as the College Chapel until 1632 when the present chapel was constructed under the direction of Dr. Matthew Wren, uncle of Christopher Wren and Master of Peterhouse 1625 - 1634. He was also Bishop of Ely and later became Master of Pembroke 1663 -1665.

Dennis Flanders's painting opposite shows the unusual position of the chapel in the centre of one side of the Court between open colonnades. It is a wonderful example of the English Baroque style, largely inspired by the *high-church* revival under Charles I and imitated by Christopher Wren at Pembroke in 1663 and Emmanuel in 1666. It incurred, however, much Puritan wrath for housing "so much Popery in so small a chapel". No small wonder that Bishop Wren was imprisoned by Parliament in the Tower for eighteen years, 1642 -1660.

PETERHOUSE

Dennis Flanders

The View across Trumpington Street

This second alternative view of the early seventeenth century Chapel was made looking across the busy Trumpington Street from the garden of the Master's Lodge, a beautiful Queen Anne House which was bequeathed to Peterhouse in 1726. Clearly seen in the picture opposite is the east window of the Chapel, which is filled with original glass which carries out a design by Rubens.

To the far right in the picture is the highly regarded Burroughs Building designed by Sir James Burroughs in 1736, undoubtedly the most elegant of his neo-Palladian buildings in Cambridge. Also, clearly shown is the pair of simple classical gateways which contrast with the towering gatehouses of colleges of the mediaeval period. They were once again the work of Sir James Burroughs in 1751.

Down either side of Trumpington Street are the mini canals known as Hobson's Conduit containing water from the Nine Wells; springs in the chalk belt three miles south of Cambridge. From 1614 until 1856 the water eventually gushed out of a fountain in Market Place. The redundant fountain-head now stands as a monument on the corner of Trumpington Street and Lensfield Road. Hobson's Conduit was a benefaction to Cambridge from Thomas Hobson, Mayor of Cambridge in the seventeenth century. He had the monopoly of the carrier service to London, hence the term "Hobson's Choice".

Cambridge has a long association with the United States of America and Peterhouse contains a memorial to the Reverend Godfrey Washington (1670 - 1729), a Fellow of Peterhouse and a great uncle to the first President of the United States. His family coat of arms is traditionally regarded as the origin of the Stars and Stripes of the American flag.

Hugh de Balsham, Bishop of Ely, founded the college in 1284 but did not have time to draw up the college statutes before he died in 1286. This was finally accomplished in 1338 by Simon Montague, another Bishop of Ely, and his statutes contain a remarkable provision which is not repeated in any later foundation . . . one or two of its scholars at a time are permitted to study at Oxford! They are required on oath to return to the college and give the benefit of their learnings to other scholars.

Other notable Peterhouse men include the poet Thomas Grey, Charles Babbage inventor of the first mechanical computer, Sir Frank Whittle inventor of the jet engine and Sir Christopher Cockerell inventor of the hovercraft.

Petehouse

Dennis Flanders

QUEENS' COLLEGE

Dennis Roxby Bott

The Old Main Gate

In the circumstances of its foundation Queens' College repeats the history of Clare inasmuch as its founder, Andrew Dockett, like de Bardew was a resident in the University and active in its interests. In 1446 he obtained a charter from Henry VI to incorporate a college to be named the College of St. Bernard. Dockett, however, realised that for his ambitious plans to reach fruition he would need a patron. With the help of Cardinal Beaufort he aroused the interest of the eighteen year old Queen Margaret of Anjou. After all, her husband Henry VI had founded King's seven years before, so it would seem most appropriate to found a Queen's College which she did by obtaining a new charter from her husband in 1448.

However, the Wars of the Roses and the Lancastrian fall from grace threatened the continued existence of Queen's when Edward IV deposed Henry VI in 1461. He married Elizabeth Woodville in 1464 and having been a lady-in-waiting to Margaret she was graciously pleased to assume the role of patron of Queen's in 1465, when it was founded. The interest of both Margaret the Lancastrian and Elizabeth the Yorkist was recognised in 1831 when the apostrophe was repositioned after the 's' to become Queens'.

Fortunately for Queens' Andrew Dockett its original founder and first President lived to direct its fortunes for another forty years. He began and completed, in twelve months, a court, (now called Old Court) which at the time was architecturally the best in Cambridge. It contained all the elements essential to communal life including chapel, gate-tower, library, hall and kitchen. It also incorporated a cloister and represents the first use of brick as a building material on this scale in collegiate Cambridge. It remains one of the best examples of mediaeval red brick architecture in Britain. Later Cambridge colleges, notably St. John's, made much use of red brick and it is in contrast to the stone used in mediaeval Oxford.

The view through the archway between the Old Hall and Old Kitchen is one of Dennis's favourite devices for framing his subject. In this case the view across Old Court to the Old Main Gate depicts the oldest part of the college, completed in 1448.

QUEENS' COLLEGE

Dennis Roxby Bott

Cloister Court

In the early part of the sixteenth century Queens' attracted the most eminent of intellectual luminaries. Among them were John Fisher, who had been Master of Michaelhouse in 1497 and Chancellor of the University in 1504. In 1505 he accepted the Presidency of Queens' but resigned in 1508 to concentrate on the foundation of two colleges, Christ's and St. John's. He was, however, instrumental in bringing the Dutch theologian Erasmus to Queens' in 1511 in order to introduce the teaching of Greek. He remained at Queens' for four years and during this time prepared his famous edition of the New Testament in the original Greek. Erasmus heralded the New Learning of the Renaissance which effectively brought to an end the Middle Ages.

The sixteenth century also saw, in 1537, the building of the Lodge which was to provide larger and more appropriate accommodation for the President. This building contains, on the first floor, the famous Long Gallery. Much of the building material used was purchased from the Carmelite Friary next door and in 1544, as a result of the suppression of all monastic establishments under Henry VIII, Queens' was able to purchase the Carmelite site for £36. This more than doubled the area of Queens' and provided space for future expansion.

In the painting of Cloister Court the Lodge can clearly be seen on the left resting on beams across the northern cloister. It is the only substantial half timbered college building in Cambridge although until 1911 the timbers were plaster covered.

QUEENS' COLLEGE

Dennis Roxby Bott

Wooden Bridge

It is not generally appreciated that a third successive Queen endowed Queens' College. Anne Neville, the wife of the controversial Richard III (Princes in the Tower) settled the rents of lands primarily confiscated from the Earl of Oxford. However, Henry VII after defeating Richard restored these lands to the Earl. Two gifts remained from Anne's original endowments, vestments for use in the chapel and the right to use Richard's badge, the boar's head. This is still the basis of the College's second heraldic device.

Although not quite as controversial as Richard III, Queens' Wooden Bridge is often misnamed the Mathematical Bridge and its design ascribed to Isaac

Newton. Also the misnomer arose from a fanciful idea that the bridge did not have iron screws or bolts. The original wooden bridge of the present pattern was designed and built by William Etheridge in 1749. It was rebuilt to an identical design in 1867 and again in 1904 and it has always had iron screws or bolts at its main joints.

Dennis's haunting picture of a night-time setting for the bridge was an afterthought. He had already produced a daytime view in response to a commission from the College. However, he had just returned from Venice and clearly the effect of light, water and reflections was uppermost in his mind. What more dramatic than night-time incandescence over the Cam.

ST. CATHARINE'S COLLEGE

Dennis Roxby Bott

Principal Court

St. Catherine's Hall, founded in 1473, was a sucker thrown up from the parent stem of King's College which is its immediate neighbour to the north on the other side of King's Lane. Robert Woodlark, its founder, was Provost of King's from 1452 until 1479 and had twice served as Chancellor of the University.

The college is named after Saint Catherine of Alexandria (the patron saint of scholars) who was in the fourth century tortured for her Christian beliefs. The most famous of her tortures consisted of an attempt to break her on a series of wheels with knives. (Later called Catherine wheel). The machine broke so she was beheaded. The college crest consists of a golden catherine wheel which surmounts its iron front gates which are supported by well proportioned gate posts and iron railings.

In 1860 a somewhat enigmatic inconsistency occurred when the foundation, like many others in Cambridge, adopted the appellation *College* to replace *Hall.* At the same time, however, it changed the spelling of Catherine to Catharine to align it with the Greek word *catharos* meaning pure, an attribute which the college authorities, at the time, were keen to emphasise.

The mediaeval buildings of St. Catharine's were never very impressive and were of clunch (hard chalk, no proper stone being native to the area) and by the seventeenth century were so dilapidated that it was decided to rebuild. As with Clare College where similar rebuilding was undertaken by the Grumbold family of masons, the material used was predominantly brick. The principal court was begun in 1673 and the chapel finished in 1704. It was intended that a fourth eastern side should be added to the court but money ran out. This was no bad thing, however, as it turned out because the buildings are in dark coloured brick and except in bright sunlight look rather gaunt. A fourth side would have plunged the whole court into permanent gloom.

In Dennis Roxby Bott's very pretty picture the Chapel and Hall can be clearly seen to the right with the chapel in the foreground, separated from the hall by the oriel window. On the top floor of the hall is housed the famous Sherlock Library. It is named after a former Master and Bishop of London, Dr. Thomas Sherlock. Another famous alumnus is John Addenbrooke, founder of Addenbrookes Hospital.

ST. EDMUND'S COLLEGE

Jane Carpanini

College Chapel

St. Edmund's House on Mount Pleasant occupies the site of the failed Ayerst Hostel. It was founded in 1896 by the 15th Duke of Norfolk and Baron Anatole von Hugel for the education of Roman Catholic clergy and laity from St. Edmund's College in Ware.

It was in 1895 that the ban on Roman Catholics attending university, which had been imposed by the State and the Church of England, was lifted. In 1965, after being for seventy years a hall of residence, St. Edmund's became one of the new Graduate Colleges. In 1998 it received its Royal Charter and now has full College status within the University of Cambridge.

Jane Carpanini's painting opposite shows, to great effect, the college chapel which is a Grade II listed building. It was designed by Fr. Benedict Williamson. Its original design included a nave, a high alter and six side chapels. It was opened and blessed by the Cardinal Archbishop of Westminster on 16th October, 1916 and dedicated by the Bishop of East Anglia on 25th October, 2000.

The college now admits men and women of all faiths and prides itself on being an ecumenical community. The daily worship in the College Chapel is celebrated, according to the Roman Catholic rites. However, provision is made for members of all Christian churches and other world religions to worship in St. Edmund's Chapel.

In 1992 the Tower was completed with a Japanese benefaction from the Trikyo Foundation (UK) and has provided a conference suite as well as additional student rooms. From its position on Mount Pleasant it affords fine views overlooking the City of Cambridge.

ST. JOHN'S COLLEGE

John Doyle

The Hall

Holding centre stage in John Doyle's painting of the magnificent hammer beamed Hall is a portrait of St. John's founder, Lady Margaret Beaufort. It hangs above High Table and is the work of Roland Lockey in about 1572. Lady Beaufort was a direct descendant of Edward III and mother of Henry VII and died on 29th July, 1509 having successfully completed her foundation of Christ's College in 1505. In her Will she expressed her intention to dissolve the thirteenth century Hospital of Saint John which was in a ruinous state and found on its site a college. She outlived her son, however, by two months and her only male heir was her grandson, the hubristic Henry VIII, who looked unfavourably on a project which diverted so large a sum from his inheritance. Law suits ensued and only a small part of the endowment contemplated was saved for the college by the devoted efforts of a remarkable man, John Fisher, Bishop of Rochester (1469 - 1535).

In 1497 Margaret had chosen as her confessor, John Fisher from Beverley, who was a graduate of the University and extremely active in its affairs. He was ordained in 1491 and became Master of his college, Michaelhouse (later absorbed into Trinity College) in 1496. Lady Margaret had soon realised the worth of the man - his learning, his forcefulness of character and above all his integrity and humility. In the earliest years of the sixteenth century he became Vice Chancellor of the University then Chancellor, Bishop of Rochester, the first Professor of Divinity (a foundation created by Lady Margaret) and Master of Queens' College. His influence on the pious but awesome Lady Margaret was profound and together they were responsible for the foundation of both Christ's and St. John's. After Margaret's death Fisher completed the foundation of St. John's in 1511 drawing up the college's first statutes.

Although, initially held in high esteem by Henry VIII his star waned dramatically when he first opposed Henry's divorce from Queen Katharine of Aragon and then championed the supremacy of the Church and Pope over his King. Martyrdom was inevitable and he was beheaded as a traitor in June 1535, followed a month later by his friend and fellow defender of the Pope's deity, Thomas More. Both were canonized in 1935.

John Fisher was arguably, in Cambridge's long history, its most influential presence.

ST. JOHN'S COLLEGE

John Doyle

The Great Gate

The original First Court, brick built like Queens' and not clunch (hard chalk) like Christ's, was completed in 1520 and has been much altered over time. The front range, however, facing St. John's Street and incorporating the Great Gate is very much as first built. It dominates the scene and contains the colourful coat of arms of its foundress, Lady Margaret Beaufort, above which is a statue of St. John the Evangelist after whom the college was named.

The curious beasts at either side of Lady Margaret's arms are yales, mythical heraldic creatures having elephants tails, antelopes bodies and goats heads with horns capable, mythically, of swivelling from front to back. The Beaufort family motifs of the Red Rose of Lancaster and the Portcullis can be seen either side of the yales and were much used by the Tudor dynasty, Lady Margaret's descendants

St. John's statue with his symbolic eagle at his feet is a 1662 replacement for the original which was removed by Cromwell's forces during the Civil War and subsequently lost. The eagle at St. John's feet is the traditional symbol of the saint adopted by the college so that it appears frequently on gateposts, documents and even crockery and glasses.

A statue of Lady Margaret exists above the finely carved doorway opposite the Great Gate and First Court. This door leads to the Hall and Second Court. The statue is the work of Thomas Burman and was erected in 1674.

St. John's has many notable alumni known as Johnians, including William Wordsworth, Lord Palmerston, William Wilberforce and William Cecil, Lord Burghley. The latter who was chief advisor to Elizabeth I gave much help to his beloved alma mater during difficult times.

ST. JOHN'S COLLEGE

John Doyle

College Landscape

This view by John Doyle is most unusual because it will not be at all familiar to Johnians as it was painted from the Library of Trinity College next door. From this wonderful perspective can be viewed a unique feature of St. John's. It is the only college to have two bridges spanning the Cam, The Wren Bridge and the famous Bridge of Sighs.

The so called Wren Bridge which replaced an earlier mediaeval wooden structure was completed in 1712, 40 years after the Third Court it abuts was built. Although Christopher Wren had submitted a design for a bridge at the time of the Third Court's construction it was not used. Instead Robert Grumbold, who was busy rebuilding the Clare College Old Court at the time, was engaged to build the eponymous Wren Bridge.

The Bridge of Sighs came into being because the building of New Court in the 1820's on the western side of the river Cam made it necessary to have a new crossing between it and Third Court. It was designed by Henry Hutchinson, also responsible for New Court and completed in 1831. It is far prettier than its Venetian namesake and only having in common the fact that they are both covered.

John Doyle's expansive painting captures the essence of St. John's and emphasises the fact that this college is the largest in physical size of any college in Oxford or Cambridge. From the Great Gate to the present-day back exit in Cripps Court it is nearly half a mile's walk, passing through five of the college's seven courts.

To the right of the painting can be seen the massive bulk of the Chapel tower, which is one of the dominant features of the Cambridge skyline. It was not planned to be this way because Sir George Gilbert Scott's original nineteenth century Gothic style design only included a small fleche, not the 163 feet high tower that was eventually built in 1869. After work had begun a former member of the college named Henry Hoare offered £3,000 down and £1,000 a year for five years to finance the building of a tower. This was accepted but unfortunately two years later he died in a railway accident and the college was left with a large debt.

St. John's has a distinguished tradition of religious music and has possessed a chapel choir since 1670. Today the choir is world famous through recitals, broadcasts and records. In fact John Doyle's paintings in this book have been used on the cover of recent CD releases.

ST. JOHN'S COLLEGE

John Doyle

New Court

After the end of the Napoleonic Wars, Britain's economic prosperity increased and so did the demand for university education. Between 1790 and 1859 the college grew from 120 to 370 students and by the 1820s the lack of space was becoming acute. If it was to expand the college had to build on the western side of the river Cam because it possessed no more land to the east.

Despite its original intention to get the architects to build a copy of Second Court the College, fortunately, eventually accepted a design in the romantic Gothic revival style. The architects of this design were Thomas Rickman and Henry Hutchinson. They built the largest single building so far erected by any college and did so in the face of considerable physical difficulties. The land was marshy so large baulks of timber were laid down to form a raft on which the Ketton limestone structure would safely rest. The structure has

held firm since its completion in 1831 although, it was formidably expensive; £78,000 with an additional £44,000 for interest payments. The debt was finally cleared in 1857.

New Court is a romantic dream of late mediaeval style with pinnacles, cloisters and castellations abounding everywhere. It is crowned by a Gothic cupola which has become known as the *Wedding Cake*.

Nikolaus Pevsner, the architectural historian, an Honorary Fellow of St. John's, adored what he called the *"fairy skyline"*. It is basically a classical structure with Gothic detailing particularly effective in the *"wedding cake"* cupola and the long cloister that runs along the south side of the building.

ST. JOHN'S COLLEGE

John Doyle

The Second Court

At the end of the sixteenth century nearly ninety years after its foundation in 1511, the growth of the college necessitated the building of a second court. John Doyle's painting shows the beautiful work of the London builder, Ralph Simons 1598-1602, often described as *red brick perfection*. A partner in this enterprise was Gilbert Wigg of Cambridge and all the details relating to its construction, even plans and coloured elevations, survive to this day. Even the place where bricks were to be obtained was stipulated *"Stow in Norfolk or in some other place where very good brick is to be had"*.

The western range of buildings in the Second Court contains a gate-tower with a statue of St. John's second significant female benefactor, Mary Cavendish, Countess of Shrewsbury. She was the youngest daughter of the celebrated Bess of Hardwick and it was she who agreed to pay £3,400 for the construction of the Second Court. However, she only provided £2,760 which put the college is some difficulty because the final cost rose to £3,665.

She was clearly in some financial difficulty compounded eventually by two spells of imprisonment in 1611-1615 and again in 1618. Treasonable activity was alleged and she had clearly become an implacable enemy of King James I. In 1615, however, the college revealed that she was their benefactor and in 1671 a statue to commemorate her was executed by Thomas Burman and placed in a niche in what has now become known as the Shrewsbury Tower. Her coat of arms to be seen on the tower includes the mottos of the Talbots, her husband's family, a dog and her own family, the Cavendishes, stag's head.

In John Doyle's painting looking towards the Hall with its turret and bell tower the massive presence of the nineteenth century chapel tower can clearly be seen; one of the landmarks of Cambridge. John's use of shadow in the painting produces a dramatic effect which heightens the effect of the chapel tower.

SELWYN COLLEGE

Jane Carpanini

Old Court

At the end of the nineteenth century university education was expensive so Selwyn's foundation was egalitarian; to open its doors to poorer students. It had, however, no financial endowments in the traditional sense; no wealthy founder.

It was founded by public subscription in memory of George Augustus Selwyn (1809-1878), who was educated at Eton and St. John's College, Cambridge, where he was a Fellow. He became the first and only Bishop of New Zealand and Melanezia (Islands of Western Pacific including Fiji) in 1841 and helped create that dominion. He returned to England in 1868 as Bishop of Lichfield until his death in 1878, whereupon it was proposed that a fitting memorial would be the foundation of a new college named after him.

The Selwyn Memorial Committee had as Secretary Charles John Abraham, who had been suffragan bishop to George Selwyn in both New Zealand and Lichfield. He was indefatigable in his efforts to set up the new college not least in raising money and he, more than anybody, could claim to be instrumental in Selwyn's foundation in 1882.

Selwyn's foundation charter specified that the college should make provision for those who intended to become missionaries overseas and educate the sons of clergymen. Nothing in Selwyn's charter said that only members of

the Church of England should be admitted but its first Master, Arthur Lyttelton, decreed that only members of the Church of England should gain entry. This caused much controversy because in 1856 an Act of Parliament had been passed opening up the University to Undergraduates of any religion or none. Lyttelton had been an admirer of the Oxford Movement and had been a tutor at Keble College Oxford. He was not, however, conservative by disposition, in fact, a liberal and supporter of his relation by marriage, Liberal Prime Minister William Gladstone, who incidentally made a gift of the louder of Selwyn's two chapel bells. Lyttelton was a sensible and Godly man able to call Gladstone to his aid and Cambridge University rapidly accepted him and Selwyn. Although in the early years a high proportion of the college's graduates were ordained (75%), by 1969 this had fallen to 3%.

Two other Masters of note are the second Master John Selwyn (1893-1898) son of the eponymous George and the third A. F. Kirkpatrick (1898-1907). John Selwyn had been Bishop of Malanezia in succession to his father but Fitzpatrick left a more lasting legacy. He was an ex-missionary and sea-faring man who had been disabled and could not easily stand so remained seated even for the loyal toast. Senior members to this day remain seated for the loyal toast out of no disrespect for the Sovereign but out of a custom of courtesy to a former Master.

SELWYN COLLEGE

Jane Carpanini

The View across Grange Road

In 1879 the Selwyn Memorial Committee purchased from Corpus Christi College six acres of land bordering on Grange Road at a cost of £6,111. 9s. 7d. Building began in 1880 under the direction of the Architect, Sir Arthur Blomfield.

The first buildings completed in 1882 were on the west side of the Tudor Gothic Gate and Tower and Staircase A and B. The Chapel was built in 1895 before the dining hall because it was considered to be more important. It has a fine east window by Charles Eamus Kempe, a member of the New Aesthetics (a stem from the root of the Pre-Raphaelites) which was partly paid for by donations from New Zealand.

The south range containing the Jacobean style Hall was built in 1901 to a design by the firm of architects, Grayson and Ould. The old Victorian plans by Sir Arthur Blomfield, who had died in 1899, were discarded. The Hall is a noteworthy piece of architecture and its woodwork listed in the Cambridge Inventory of the Royal Commission on Historical Monuments (1959). The woodwork at the west end of the hall comes from the eighteenth century English church of St. Mary in Rotterdam which was demolished in 1913.

A. C. Benson, the Master of Magdalene College, bought the woodwork and presented it to the college in memory of his father, the archbishop, who dedicated Selwyn's Chapel. A distinctive feature of the Hall is the fine balustraded stone staircase at the entrance. It contains the initials F.S.M. prankishly carved, along with those of other undergraduates, on a course of bricks near the north east angle. F.S.M. are those of F. S. Marsh, who later became a Fellow of Selwyn, eminent orientalist and Lady Margaret Professor of Divinity; the first Selwyn man to be a Professor of the University in 1944.

In Jane Carpanini's painting on the previous page the Chapel can clearly be seen on the left and the Hall on the far right with the stone steps clearly visible. On the opposite page is a view across Grange Road of Selwyn's first buildings with the castellated Gate and Tower entrance in the centre.

Incidentally the coat of arms shown at the top of this page is an amalgam of the Selwyn family arms and those of the Diocese of Lichfield, where George Augustus Selwyn was Bishop for ten years until his death in 1878.

SIDNEY SUSSEX COLLEGE

John Doyle

Chapel Court

The foundation of Sidney Sussex College in 1596 marks the end of an era. It was the sixteenth college to be founded in Cambridge in just over three hundred years and there would not be another until Downing in 1800.

Like five previous Cambridge colleges Sidney Sussex was founded by a noble lady, Frances Sidney, Countess of Sussex, who was also the aunt of the romantic soldier and poet, Sir Philip Sidney. When she died in 1589 her Will specified that a sum of £5,000 plus the residue of her estate, after specific bequests should be applied in founding a college to be called The Lady Frances Sidney Sussex College. Her Executors, Henry Gray, Earl of Kent, and Sir John Harrington were appointed to supervise the work of founding and giving to the college its first statutes. The Sidney statutes contain all the puritan zeal of Emmanuel founded twelve years earlier, exhibiting the Elizabethan abhorrence and detestation of "Popery".

As in the case of Emmanuel the site chosen for Sidney had previously been occupied by a house of mendicants (itinerant friars) in this case Franciscans. In 1546 the Friary had been suppressed and its six acre site and buildings appropriated by Henry VIII to assist with the foundation of his own college, Trinity. Most of the buildings were dismantled and their stones used in the construction of Trinity. Trinity resisted the attempts of Frances Sidney's

Executors to acquire the, by now, derelict site and it took the intervention of Elizabeth I to persuade the Trinity men to lease the site to Sidney in perpetuity for an annual rent of 20 marks (£13 6s. 8d.). The payment of this annual sum has continued to the present day.

Having secured the site Lady Sidney's Executors moved with great alacrity appointing as builder, Ralph Simons who had earlier worked at St. John's and Emmanuel. He utilised the only remaining building from the Friary days, the partly demolished refectory which was used to house a chapel on the ground floor and a library above. With the same perversity as at Emmanuel the chapel was turned north - south. Other brick buildings were constructed and by 1598 Simons had completed not only the Chapel but also, to the north, Hall Court which contained the Kitchen, Hall and Master's Lodge. Chapel Court was not actually completed until the mid seventeenth century, when the third side was built.

John Doyle's unusual view of Chapel Court was painted from the third floor of an architect's office opposite the college. Many artists would shy clear of thrusting their presence upon a third party in this way but not John; he is a great ambassador for the arts.

SIDNEY SUSSEX COLLEGE

John Doyle

The College Gatehouse

By the middle of the eighteenth century Sidney's buildings were becoming seriously dilapidated. In 1774 James Essex designed a new chapel which replaced Ralph Simon's earlier building. The Old Chapel was demolished in 1776 and the new building completed in 1782 contained at the southern end the new Chapel and at the northern end, on the first floor, the College Library (now called the Old Library). The Chapel was extended in 1920s and given elaborate oak panelled walls and a variegated marble floor.

The present appearance of Sidney is due to the extensive remodelling it received in the 1820s by Sir Jeffrey Wyatt. He removed the classical gateway replacing it with a new porter's lodge and tower. He covered the red brick buildings with Roman cement adding a porch and bell-turret to the chapel and gables and battlements in the Gothic manner. The result was a more homogenous appearance which has at times come in for some sharp criticism although it finds itself fashionable again today.

The best known member of the college was Oliver Cromwell, who came up in 1616 but left after one year to support his family following his father's death. After the execution of Charles I in 1649 Cromwell became Lord Protector of England. After the restoration of the monarchy in 1660

Cromwell's body was exhumed, hanged and beheaded. His head was impaled on a pole in Westminster Hall where it remained for twenty years, until a great storm blew it down. It then had a varied and well documented career and spent part of its time as a fairground attraction - "pay sixpence and see Oliver's head". In 1960, however, it was presented to the college by Dr. H. N. S. Wilkinson and was buried in a secret place in the ante-chapel in the presence of the Master and two Fellows. His death-mask can be found in the Old Library and there is, in the Senior Common Room, a pastel portrait by Samuel Cooper which, like Sir Peter Lely's famous portrait, shows Cromwell *"warts and all"*. A very good oil painting of Oliver Cromwell from the late seventeenth century by an artist unknown, but after the style of Lely, hangs in the Hall. It was known to have belonged to Cromwell's son, Richard and came into the possession of the College about seventy years ago as a gift of a Master.

John Doyle has once again managed to surprise with his ingenious view looking from Chapel Court through the gate-tower towards Hall Court. Sidney is unusual inasmuch as its two principal Courts which are shown in John's painting are three sided; their fourth range is separated from Sidney Street by a brick wall.

TRINITY COLLEGE

Dennis Flanders

The Great Court

When Henry VIII founded Trinity in 1546 he amalgamated two earlier foundations. Michaelhouse and King's Hall and also secured their lucrative endowments. Very little architecturally remains of Michaelhouse on the present Trinity site. However, the Chapel of Michaelhouse still remains in Trinity Street, having been converted into the Michaelhouse Centre, a multi-purpose functions facility, including a café. Much more is left of King's Hall including Trinity's two finest gateways. The Great Gate and Edward III's gate-tower.

Dennis Flanders's fine painting of The Great Court (the largest quadrangle in either Oxford or Cambridge) looking northwards captures its grandeur which has the appearance of having been designed at one time and by a single mind. As a matter of fact it is the outcome of one hundred and fifty years evolution and the buildings which it contains range from the reign of Edward III (mid fourteenth century) to James I (late sixteenth century). King Edward's gate-tower with its famous clock and statue of Edward III can be seen at the top of Dennis's painting with the chapel on the right, which was built by Mary I soon after her accession. King Edward's gate-tower had originally stood about 70 feet to the south of its present position where the sundial now stands. It was moved to its present position by Thomas Neville (Master 1593-1615) a very rich man who wanted to enlarge the court to its present size, which covers just over two acres.

To the right of the painting is the Great Gate which is now the main entrance to the college and contains on its inner side statues of James I, his Queen Anne of Denmark and his son Prince Charles. Thomas Neville was responsible for much of the architectural splendour which makes Trinity pre-eminent among Cambridge colleges. He began the Dining Hall in 1601 and it remains not only the largest dining hall in Cambridge but is one of the finest examples of a great Elizabethan Hall. The steps to the hall can be seen on the left of Flanders's picture.

Neville's crowning glory and Trinity's in the centre of the court is the fountain erected in 1602. Its supply of water which has been continuous since 1325 comes from a spring three miles to the west of Cambridge. It originally flowed to a Franciscan Friary (where Sidney Sussex College now stands) which was abandoned at the time of Henry VIII's Dissolution of the Monasteries (see page 98) and thereby providing Trinity with a ready supply of water. To complete the symmetry of his Great Court Neville built a third gate-tower, the Queen's Gate which stands in the middle of the south range and contains a statue of Queen Elizabeth I.

Regularly over the years students have attempted to dash around the Great Court in the 43 seconds it takes the clock on King Edward's gate-tower to strike 12 o'clock. Not many have succeeded.

TRINITY COLLEGE

Dennis Roxby Bott

The Great Gate

In 1545 Henry VIII passed an act for the dissolution of the colleges in the same manner as monasteries earlier and vesting their property in the King and his successors. In moving terms the University petitioned Queen Katherine Parr to use her influence with the King who was dying. His heart was stirred with pity for the poverty of the University. He not only halted the dissolution but made noble reparation by founding Trinity. The King's scheme was to establish a college on a scale even grander than that of King's in Cambridge and Christ Church, Oxford. In wealth and magnificence it was to be second to none. It was to be a symbol of the emancipation of the English Church from the control of Rome and to acknowledge the King as its earthly head.

Therefore, in 1546 three ancient institutions were combined to form the new Trinity College, Michaelhouse (1324), King's Hall (1337) and Physick Hostel which was appropriated from Gonville Hall. The present gate-tower entrance shown in the painting opposite was completed in 1535 and was part of King's Hall and contained a statue of Edward III, its founder. However, his statue was replaced by one of Henry VIII after Trinity's takeover of King's Hall, although interestingly the coat of arms of Edward III and his six sons still remain immediately below Henry's statue.

To the right of the Great Gate in Dennis Roxby Bott's painting and connecting to the chapel is a small range of buildings which contained the rooms occupied by Sir Isaac Newton from 1679-1696. The lawn in front of these buildings contained a great garden referred to as Newton's garden. In the painting can be seen the apple tree planted in 1954 which is directly descended from the one at Newton's home, Woolthorpe Manor, near Grantham, which is traditionally associated with his discovery of the force of gravity.

In 1661, aged 18, Newton entered Trinity somewhat ignominiously as a sub-sizar. This meant that in return for financial assistance he had to perform certain menial functions. He obtained a B.A. degree in 1665 and was elected a Fellow in 1667. In the next twenty years he advanced the state of mathematical knowledge to such an extent that it took other mathematicians another 50 years to take it all in.

In 1696 he removed to London where he was elected, in 1702, President of the Royal Society a post he held until his death in 1727. His statue by Roubiliacs can be seen in the central space of Trinity's ante-chapel. It is considered to be one of the few really first class pieces of monumental architecture in Cambridge.

TRINITY COLLEGE

Dennis Roxby Bott

Wren's Library from The Backs

To the west and behind The Hall Thomas Neville, who was appointed Master of Trinity by Elizabeth I in 1593, built his eponymous Neville's Court with its famous cloisters. Above the cloisters in the western range of the court is the College Library, the finest building in Trinity. It was not built by Neville but a later Master, Isaac Barrow (Master 1672-1677), who was a great friend of Sir Christopher Wren. He persuaded Wren to design a library to sit above the cloisters, which he did and gave his services *gratis*.

Christopher Wren modelled the Trinity Library on that of St. Marks in Venice. It cost £16,000 and measured 200 feet long, 42 feet wide and 37 feet high. The book-cases were made by a Cambridge carpenter with limewood carvings by Grinling Gibbons. Wren was as much interested in the interior as in the exterior of the building and he designed the tall shelves down the sides and even the furniture in the alcoves. The white busts of Trinity's eminent men on Wren's pedestals at the end of the book-cases are mostly by

Roubiliac. The statue of Byron by Thorwaldsen was originally intended for Westminster Abbey but it was declined and languished for twelve years at the Customs House before the College provided a home for their former student.

Among the many treasured possessions contained in the library are manuscripts such as Milton's "Paradise Lost", Tennyson's "In Memoriam" and Macauley's Diary as well as Edwin's Psalter, written at Canterbury in 1150. Close to the Byron statue on the west (river) side the last alcove contains Isaac Newton's private library presented to the college by the Pilgrim's Trust.

Dennis Roxby Bott's painting from the Backs (as grounds on either side of the river Cam are called) is an unusual view of Wren's Library as it is normally portrayed from Neville's Court with integral cloisters.

TRINITY HALL

Dennis Roxby Bott

Trinity Lane Front

In the late 1340's England, like the rest of Europe, was devastated by the Black Death and in the ninety years which followed a third of its population succumbed. William Bateman, the Bishop of Norwich lost almost 700 of his parish priests and it prompted him, in 1350, to found The Hall of the Holy Trinity of Norwich, to educate students in the canon and civil law. In the fourteenth century the studies of Theology and Law, especially Canon Law, was recognised as a necessary prerequisite to high attainment in the Church. Trinity Hall was founded on a plot of land which had previously been occupied by a hostel of Benedictine monks from Ely.

It has always been difficult to get a decent perspective of this famous law college. Its front entrance opens onto an ancient lane once known in mediaeval times as Milne Street but now called Trinity Lane and its narrowness defeats even the wide angle lens. It takes a truly gifted topographical draughtsman to achieve a creditable perspective. This Roxby Bott has done, capturing the essence of this quaint corner of Cambridge whose cobbled lane connects Trinity College to King's College, passing the colleges of Trinity Hall, Gonville and Caius and Clare on the way.

Interestingly Trinity Hall's name may appear to be an anachronism because although in the mediaeval period the first colleges were called halls, as in halls of residence, by the nineteenth century most of the old halls, such as Pembroke

Hall and St. Catharine's Hall had adopted the appellation, *college*, to indicate the integral presence of scholars. Such a change in the case of Trinity Hall was impossible because a Trinity College already existed, albeit nearly two hundred years its junior. Thus, uniquely amongst the mediaeval colleges of Cambridge, it retains its old name.

The entrance screen of Trinity Hall, seen to the right of the picture, was designed by Anthony Salvin in the 1850s to replace Sir James Burrough's short lived eighteenth century building which had been destroyed by fire in 1850, along with most of the front court.

To the left in Roxby Bott's painting can be seen part of Cockerell Building, constructed in 1842 to house the rapidly expanding University Library. To the right of this building is the projecting oriel of the Old Schools, the administrative core of the University of Cambridge since 1350. It also contains, but not visible in the painting, the gatehouse which dates from 1441 and was the entrance to King's Old Court which was, until the eighteenth century, the only secular part of King's College. On completion of King's Front Court on King's Parade, in the early nineteenth century, Old Schools acquired the redundant Old Court of King's and its gatehouse was heavily restored and extended by George Gilbert Scott in 1867.

WOLFSON COLLEGE

Dennis Flanders

The Main Entrance

The University of Cambridge founded University College in 1965 to cater for the needs of graduates from other universities who were coming to Cambridge to engage in further study or to do research.

In 1973 University College changed its name to Wolfson College in recognition of a major benefaction from the Wolfson Foundation (created by Scottish philanthropist Isaac Wolfson) of £2m. This provided additional buildings which form an E shape on a thoughtfully laid out site. Interestingly the floor of the main entrance hall (situated in the white building at the centre of the picture opposite) is made of thin slices of granite taken from the old London Bridge.

Though begun as a post graduate institution Wolfson now gives over 20% of its places to undergraduates. These students like all others in Cambridge take a "Tripos" which is the name given to the examination leading to a first degree B.A. or Batchelor of Arts. Tripos is taken from the Greco-Latin for a three legged stool and refers to the object on which the examiner used to sit in the days of oral examinations. Tripos is unique to Cambridge and in this context has been in use since the sixteenth century. Incidentally after a six years residence at Cambridge University a student becomes eligible for a Master of Arts degree, M.A.

Wolfson celebrated its Silver Jubilee in July 1990 and decided to commemorate this landmark by commissioning a painting by Dennis Flanders from which limited edition prints would be made and offered for sale to past students. It also coincided with the appointment of Wolfson's President, David Williams as Vice Chancellor of the University.

A distinctive feature of Wolfson College is its truly international flavour with a very large proportion of post graduate students coming from overseas. At the time of its Silver Jubilee out of a total of 2,800 past students 1,500 were from overseas. It is hardly surprising, therefore, that the college has an unsurpassed world wide reputation.

Wolfson College

Dennis Flanders.